Joe Pauker

GET LOST!

The Cool Guide to Amsterdam

Get Lost Publishing, 1995

CIP-gegevens Koninklijke Bibliotheek, Den Haag

Pauker, Joe

Get Lost! : The Cool Guide To Amsterdam / Joe Pauker ;
[ed. Lisa Kristensen]. - Amsterdam : Get Lost Publishing.
- Ill., foto's, plgr.
1e dr.: Amsterdam : Pauker, 1994
ISBN 90-802561-1-0
NUGI 471
Trefw.: Amsterdam ; reisgidsen

© Joe Pauker, 1995

For all their help, advice and support, many thanks to ... Albert, Ashka, Barak, Clivir, Dion, Doug, Elsbeth, Ettle Bettle, Henk, Ian, Kate, Klaus, Laura, Mary, Michel, Niala, Susan, Willem... and most of all, Lisa.

Research assistance and editing by Lisa Kristensen
Editor's note: I know how to use capital letters, but this author is an Artist (like e.e.cummings).

Cover by Ellen von Pauker

Layout by Chris Stevenet

Printing by Drukkkerij PAL

Central map based on one from Stedelijk Beheer Amsterdam, Landmeten en Vastgoedinformatie, afd. Kartografie

Printed on 100% recycled paper

Cover stock (25% hemp/75% recycled) from Alma Rosa, Handelslei 12, 2960 Brecht, Belgium. Tel: 323-281-4595. Fax: 323-281-4596

INTRODUCTION

Welcome to the coolest, hippest, most happening city in Europe. And to this new edition of Get Lost! I wrote the first edition three years ago. I wanted it to include the things that I look for when I visit a new city: places that often aren't in other guides. I borrowed a friend's computer, learned WordPerfect as I worked, and spent a week typing up my hand-written manuscript. When I returned the computer (this is a true story), my friend plugged it in and it blew up!

I published the first edition of The Cool Guide at a squat printer and distributed it with the help of friends. It sold out. So did the second edition. This third edition has been completely revised and updated. It continues to be an independent, DIY project. I've sold a few ads to help me pay for the printing, but most of the money comes from my own pocket. Nobody pays to be in this book, and you will never see an ad from a big beer or cigarette company in Get Lost! Unfortunately, this means that I have to work at several shit jobs too. But I do have a fun time researching and writing Get Lost! and I hope that it's reflected in the text.

This year we finally got hemp paper for the cover and hopefully next year will see the entire book printed on tree-free hemp paper. Thanks for buying Get Lost! Have a cool time!

P.S. I've tried to be very accurate with regard to prices, opening times, etc., but I'm just a goof and things change. Feel free to write if you have any suggestions, complaints, or spare change. If you want to mail order a copy, send well concealed cash or an International **Postal** Money Order for $10 US (sorry, no cheques) made out to Get Lost!

Get Lost!
c/o Galerie
Reestraat 25
1016 DM, Amsterdam
The Netherlands

COMING SOON:
Get Lost! The Cool Guide To Amsterdam (German Edition)
Get Lost! The Cool Guide To Cape Town

CONTENTS

PLACES TO SLEEP 7
    Hostels 8
    Hotels 10
    Camping 12

GETTING AROUND 13
    Bicycles 13
    Recumbent Bikes 14
    Inline Skates 15
    Mopeds 15
    Public Transport 15
    Taxis 16
    Boat Tours 16
    Motor Boats 17
    Canal Bikes 17

GETTING OUT OF AMSTERDAM 18
    Bus 18
    Hitching 18
    Travellers' Bulletin Board 19
    Air Travel 19
    Getting to the Beach 20
    Getting To The Airport 20

PRACTICAL SHIT 21
    Changing Money 21
    Telephone 21
    Post Office 22

FOOD 23
    Supermarkets 23
    Health Food Stores 24
    Tropical Shops 24
    Street Foods 25
    Night Shops 26
    All Night Eating 26
    Sundays 27
    Free Samples 27
    Breakfast 27
    Restaurants 28

CAFÉS 35

CANNABIS 40
   Coffeeshops 41
   Seeds/Grow Shops 46

SHOPPING 50
   Markets 50
   Books & Magazines 52
   Records, Tapes & CDs 55
   Club Fashions 56
   Miscellaneous 57

HANGING OUT 62
   Vondelpark 62
   Leidseplein 62
   Dam Square 62
   Library 63
   Snooker 63
   Virgin Megastore 63
   Gardens 64
   Hoops 64
   Skateboarding 64
   Kite Flying 65
   Sauna 65

MUSEUMS 66
   The Big Ones 69

MUSIC 70
   How To Find Out Who's Playing 70
   Live Music/Party Venues 71
   Dance Clubs 74
   Radio 75
   Steet music 75
   Festivals 76

BARS 79

FILM 83

SEX 85
   Sex Shops 86
   Peep Shows And Live Sex 88
   Miscellaneous Sex Stuff 89

DICTIONARY 91

PHONE NUMBERS 92
   Emergency and Health 92
   General Info Lines 94
   Embassies 94

About The Author

Joe Pauker was born in a muddy field at Woodstock while Jimi Hendrix played "The Star Spangled Banner". His parents, both members of The Weather Underground, were accidentally killed in an explosion in Greenwich Village. He was adopted by members of the People's Church and moved to Guyana to live with the Rev. Jim Jones. Joe escaped the Kool-aid massacre by fleeing into the jungle where he was raised by apes. After being discovered by missionaries the young boy was sent to New York City to live with his aunt, a roadie for the Ramones. In the early 90's he moved to Amsterdam where he worked as a stripper. In May 1995, just after completing this edition of Get Lost, he was murdered by an English soccer hooligan.

PLACES TO SLEEP

Although there is an abundance of luxury hotel rooms (most sitting vacant), there just aren't enough cheap hotel rooms for all the visitors to Amsterdam, especially in the summer. It can be a real drag finding a place to stay, and if you're in town for just a few days you don't want to waste time, so here are a few hints to help you out.

One of your best bets is to go with a "runner" (someone who has the shitty job of running back and forth between a hotel and the train station). Some of these people work for hotels or hostels with less than 5 rooms (these small hotels can't register with the tourist information centre), or for private homes and guest houses. A lot of the runners carry books with photos of the rooms so you can look at what you're getting. I've found some really great places this way. I've also seen some dives, but it doesn't cost to look.

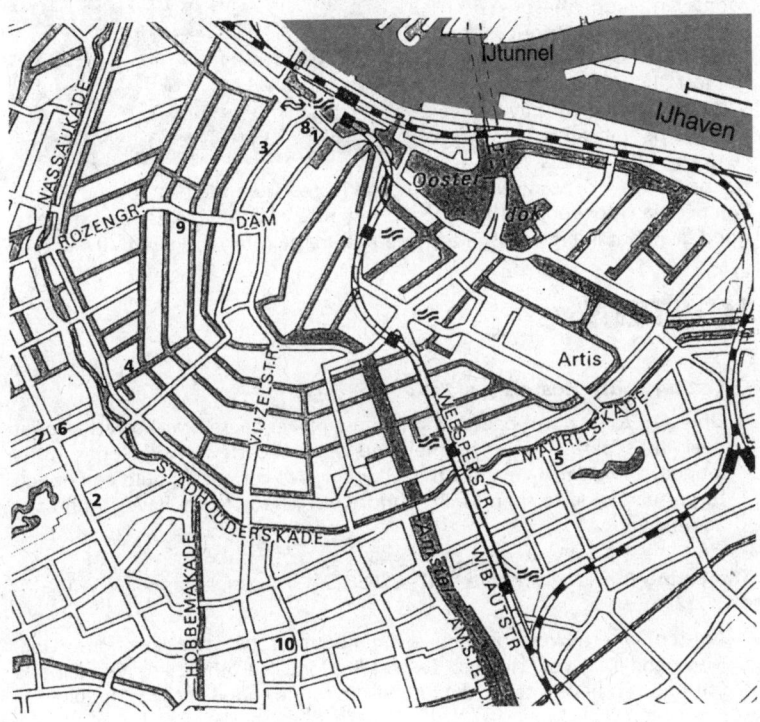

In the summer a bed in a hostel runs anywhere from ƒ15-ƒ30 and a clean double room for less than ƒ100 is a good deal. In the winter in never hurts to bargain a little and double rooms can be found for ƒ60-ƒ70.

At the VVV tourist office (across the square in front of Central Station and to your left) they have a room finding service. They can book you a dorm bed at a cheaper price, but plain double rooms in high season start at f100 (without bath) and of course these go fast. If you use the VVV you have to pay them ƒ5 per person service charge and another ƒ5 per person as a deposit (which is later deducted from the price of the room). The people who work at the VVV are very nice and sometimes you can get a good deal, but in high season the line-ups are painfully long and slow.

HOSTELS

Christian Youth Hostels

Only ƒ15 for a dorm bed and breakfast makes these two hostels a great deal. But separate rooms for men and women, curfews, sing-alongs in the lounge, and a clean-cut staff that's looking for converts should be enough to persuade you to spend a little more elsewhere. You'll have to find the address yourself.

The Flying Pig - *Nieuwendijk 100, 420-6822 (1), Vossiusstraat 46-47, 400-4187 (2)*

Amsterdam's newest budget accommodation has two locations. One, Nieuwendijk, is very close to Central Station. The other is by Vondelpark. Both hostels have a total of 130 beds: in single rooms for ƒ85; doubles for

Hostels

ƒ100; and shared rooms with 4 beds ƒ33.50, 6 beds ƒ30, 8 beds ƒ28, 10 beds ƒ25.50 (per person). Look for a drop, off season, of about 10%. All rooms have toilets and showers. Nieuwendijk has a TV in every room and a bar that opens at midnight and stays open until 08:00. That's cool. It's also right next door to the Twin Pigs Café which has live music most nights (no cover), and a 2 for 1 happy hour (18-19:00). The guys who run these places are travellers themselves, which explains such things as the free use of kitchens to prepare your own food, and the absence of curfews. On checking in, you get a coupon for a free beer at the in-house bar. That's cool, too. Both sites are central, but the neighbourhood around Vondelpark is much nicer. To reach Vossiusstraat from Central Station take tram 1, 2, 5 or 11 to Leidseplein. Walk over the bridge to Vondelpark. The street runs along the left side of the park.

Bob's Youth Palace - *Nieuwezijds Voorburgwal 92, 623-0063 (3)*

You can usually find this hostel by looking for a bunch of people sitting on the front steps smoking joints and strumming guitars. This is a pretty cool, clean place where a lot of travellers stay. It's right in the centre of the city and the ƒ22 gets you a dorm bed and breakfast. You can walk from the station; it's not far.

International Budget Hotel - *Leidsegracht 76, 624-2784 (4)*

This place is in a couple of other guide books too, but I recommend it because I spent a few nights here once and liked it. The rooms aren't beautiful, but they're clean, and if you're going to stay in a dorm it's nice that there are only 4 beds to a room. There's also a comfortable lounge with a tv and videos that you can rent, but when I was there the staff were playing them for free (oops, maybe I shouldn't have said that). Finally, everyone I met working there was really friendly and that's important. A bed in a 4 person dorm is f30 and there are a couple of double rooms with tv for ƒ110. Cheaper rates off season. From Central Station take tram 1,2, or 5 to Leidseplein and then it's a short walk. Also owned by the same folks is the Euphemia Budget Hotel at Fokke Simonszstraat 1 (622-9045). They've done nice renovations there and have some double rooms for ƒ90 (ƒ120 with shower and toilet). A 4 person dorm is ƒ35 pp.

Sleepin-ARENA - *'s-Gravesandestraat 51-53, 694-7444 (5)*

I first stayed in this huge, old mansion 13 years ago and I still think it's one of the coolest hostels in town. Its main drawback, being a bit out of the centre, is made up for by the fact that with 600 beds and great facilities the Sleepin is often a happening place in itself. The whole building has recently been renovated. There's a games room, a restaurant/bar (see Restaurant section), and a really nice concert-hall (see Music section). In the summer they have a coffeeshop and you can also rent bicycles. And where else can you share a dorm with 75 other people for only ƒ20 a night? Smaller dorms with 4-8 people sharing go for ƒ32.50 per person. There are also women-only dorms in high season, and double and triple rooms (see Hotels, this section). From Central Station take tram 3,6,9,10, or 14 to Mauritskade. Night bus 76 or 77.

HOTELS

Here are a few places with clean, reasonably priced rooms. In the summer you should really try to arrange your accommodation before leaving Central Station, through a runner, the VVV, or by calling one of the hotels below.

Hotel Princess - *Overtoom 80, 612-2947 (6)*

This hotel is at a busy intersection about a five minute walk from Leidseplein. It's just been refurbished and the owner has added lots of nice touches like reading lights by the bed, and mirrors. Single rooms are ƒ60-80. Doubles start at ƒ90 and go up to ƒ125 for rooms with a private shower and toilet. Breakfast is included and it's excellent: bread, cheese, ham, cereal, boiled eggs, juice and coffee. The rest of the day drinks and snacks are available at the reception. The staff are very nice, but unfortunately the sexy guy with the cool dreads is gone. Tram 1 from Central Station to Constantijn Huygensstraat.

Hotel Abba - *Overtoom 122, 618-3058 (7)*

This is another hotel with friendly, helpful staff. An all you can eat breakfast in a sunny room is included. Singles ƒ70. Doubles with shower and toilet range from ƒ100 to ƒ120. Most of the rooms are okay, but some are a bit dingy and have no reading lights, so you should ask to see the room first. By this summer all the rooms should be refurbished. If you're staying for awhile they have some two room apartments with kitchens for ƒ200-ƒ240 that are good for 4 to 6 people. In winter there is a serious drop in price, sometimes up to 30% off the prices listed here. Close to Leidseplein and Vondelpark. Tram 1 from Central Station to Constantijn Huygensstraat.

The Flying Pig - *Nieuwendijk 100, 420-6822 (1), Vossiusstraat 46-47, 400-4187 (2)*

Both these hostels have double rooms with shower and toilet for ƒ100. The Nieuwendijk rooms even have TV's. It's a very good deal. Singles are ƒ85. See Hostels, above for more details.

Groenendael - *Nieuwendijk 15, 624-4822 (8)*

If you prefer to stay closer to the centre of town, then this hotel is a good deal. Singles go for ƒ60, doubles for ƒ85, and triples for ƒ40 per person (cheaper off season). Showers and toilets are in the hall. Breakfast is included. Some rooms have showers for about ƒ10 more. The rooms are pretty basic, but you're paying for the location. There's a comfortable lounge to hang out in and meet people. From Central Station walk or run.

Sleepin ARENA - *'s Gravesandestraat 51, 694-7444 (5)*

I already mentioned this place in the Hostels section, but I didn't say that they now have 40 double rooms with shower and toilet for only ƒ90! This is a really good deal if you don't mind staying a bit out of the centre. No breakfast included. However, all rooms have reading lights by the beds: the mark of a good hotel. Triple rooms with shower and toilet are ƒ125. A ƒ40 key deposit is returned when you check out. Make a reservation. Close to the Tropenmuseum. From Central Station take tram 3,6,9,10, or 14 to Mauritskade. Night bus 76 or 77.

Hotel Aspen - *Raadhuisstraat 31, 626-6714 (9)*

A nice-sized, double room with shower and toilet is ƒ100. Doubles with sink only are ƒ75-ƒ80. Triples go for ƒ30-ƒ40 per person with shower and toilet. No breakfast, but a great location close to Dam Square and Anne Frank House. From Central Station take tram 13 or 17 to Westermarkt and walk back half a block. If you don't have much luggage, it's only a 10-15 minute walk.

Van Ostade Bicycle Hotel - *Van Ostadestraat 123, 679-3452 (10)*

If you're travelling by bicycle take note. This is the only hotel in Amsterdam with indoor bike parking! This unique service will only set you back an extra ƒ2.50 a night: a steal in this city of bike thieves. They also rent bikes to guests for ƒ7.50 per day and provide info on tours in and out of Amsterdam. The rooms? ƒ90 for a double with sink, ƒ125.00 for a double with shower and TV. Breakfast included. The rooms aren't exciting, but clean. Library/lounge downstairs. Close to Albert Cuyp market. Take tram 24 or 25 from Central Station to Ceintuurbaan and then walk one block.

Hotel Strips

Walking around and looking for a hotel can be a pain, but if you really want to, here are a few areas with clusters of hotels, which should make it a little easier for you.

Raadhuisstraat - The beautiful art nouveau Utrecht building is located just east of the Westerkerk and is full of small reasonably priced hotels. I stopped in at the Hotel Aspen (see above). These hotels fill up fast.

Warmoesstraat - You'll find several hostels and hotels here at the edge of the red light district. Some of them are dives and others, like the Hotel Kabul (tel: 623 7158) have been around a long time and have a good reputation.

Haarlemmerstraat - This area is close to Central Station and has a selection of hotels and hostels. Some, but not all, are pretty scummy, so check the room before you pay.

Damrak - I wouldn't stay along here unless I had lots of money, in which case I'd go to the Victoria Hotel and book into the room out of which Chet Baker jumped. (R.I.P.)

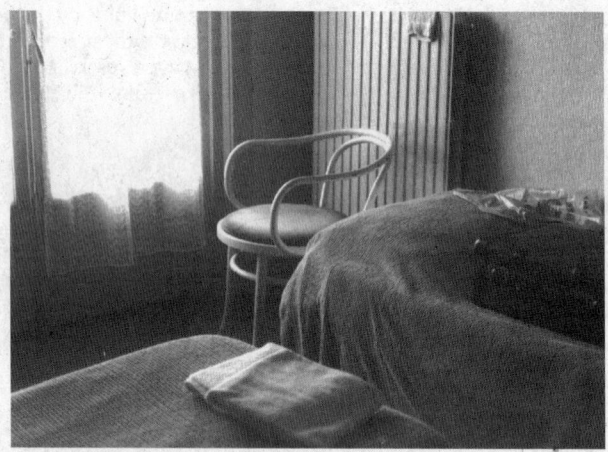

Somebody **died** in this room.

CAMPING

Vliegenbos - *Meeuwenlaan 138, 636-8855*

ƒ9 per person; ƒ10.50 if you're over 30 years old. There are also charges for vehicles. New this year are 30 cabins (four beds each) for ƒ61.50. Open 1 April - 30 September. Bus 32, 36, 39. Night bus 72.

Zeeburg - *IJdijk 44, 694-4430*

ƒ6.25 per person plus ƒ3.25 for tent. Open all year. Metro to Amstel Station, then bus 37, then a 2 minute walk. Night bus 71 (20 minute walk)

GETTING AROUND

Central Amsterdam's old cobblestone streets are great for wandering through and getting lost. Fortunately, Amsterdam is full of people who speak English (to get you found). But you shouldn't have too much trouble if you take few minutes to study a map. Amsterdam Diamond Center (Rokin 1-5) gives away free maps of the city centre. More detailed maps are available all over. Buy one: they're only ƒ3.50 and the street names listed on the back will make it fast and easy to find the places mentioned in this book.

The basic layout of the city, with a series of horseshoe shaped canals surrounding the oldest part, makes it fairly easy to find your way on foot. This is certainly the best way to see Amsterdam and fully appreciate its incredible beauty.

BICYCLES

Don't be scared to rent a bike and go for an authentic Amsterdam experience. Unlike most North American and many European cities, bikes are respected in Amsterdam. Dirty, ugly, polluting cars are slowly being forced out of the city centre, in favour of beautiful, clean, fast, efficient bicycles. There are bike lanes all over the city and it's a fun, safe way to explore Amsterdam. Listed below are several places to rent bikes. If you're here for awhile you may want to consider buying a used bike and selling it back to a shop when you leave. Make sure you lock your bike everywhere, even if you're only leaving it for an instant (see note on bike theft).

Rent-A-Bike-Damstraat - *Pieterjacobszdwarsstraat 11, 625-5029*
In an alley off Damstraat just east of Dam Square. Very friendly. ƒ10 per day, but the more days you rent the cheaper it gets. Their special weekly rate is ƒ50. ƒ50 deposit plus passport or credit card. Open every day 09-18:00.

Bike City - *Bloemgracht 70, 626-3721*
Another very friendly shop. Located on a beautiful canal near Anne Frank House. Rental includes a puncture repair kit with instructions (a bonus if you're heading for the countryside). ƒ10 per day, which means 09-18:00. ƒ50 deposit plus passport or credit card. Open daily 09-18:00.

Macbike - *Marnixstraat 220, 626 6964, Nieuwe Uilenburgstraat 16, 620 0985*
Good quality bikes and a good reputation. ƒ10 per day plus ƒ50 and passport or credit card. Special weekly rate, ƒ55. Open every day 09-18:00.

Take-A-Bike - *Stationplein, 624-8391*
Out the main doors at Central Station and to your left. Cheap, but kinda sleazy. ƒ8.00 per day plus ƒ200 deposit plus passport. Special weekly rate ƒ32. Open mon-fri 06-22:00, sat 07-22:00, sun 08-22:00.

Frederic Rent A Bike - *Brouwersgracht 78, 624-5509*
Only 5 minutes from Central Station. Also opening a Vondelpark location this spring. ƒ10 per day, which means 09-18:00 in the summer and 24 hours off season. Open daily 09-18:00.

De Rommelmarkt - *Looiersgracht 38*
There's a big tree by the entrance to this flea market (see Markets, Shopping section), that often has a few used bikes leaning against it. You might find something for about ƒ50. Wed and sat are the best days to check. Open 11-17:00.

Binnenpret - *1e Schinkelstraat 14*
My apologies to anyone who bought a bike here last year after reading my recommendation. I was so happy and excited at finding a place to buy used bikes at a cheap price. Then I bought two (two!) bikes here and they were both shit. So, I'm sorry.

RECUMBENT BIKES

Fancy Frames - *1e van Swindenstraat 553, 694-6448*
By now you must have seen someone riding one of these bikes, low to the ground with their feet stretched out in front and bodies laying back in a chair-like seat. Now you can rent one! I tried one the other day and it was amazing. It's a bit wobbly at first, but once you get the hang of it they are quite comfortable, and fast. You can rent them for a half day for ƒ20, but because they would be more fun in the open spaces of the countryside, a whole day for ƒ35 would probably make more sense. The price includes insurance. Open tues-sat 09-17:00 (thurs 'til 21:00).

INLINE SKATES

Rodolfo's - *Sarphatistraat 59, 622-5488*
Magna Plaza, Nieuwezijds Voorburgwal 182, 623-1214

Roller blades for rent! Skating is good on the bike lanes and the people who work here know all the hot spots around town. The rental is from 12 noon to 12 noon and the price is ƒ15. ƒ300 deposit or credit card. They also sell snowboards, skateboards and skate fashions. Open mon 13-18:00, tues-fri 10-18 (thurs 19-21:00 too), sat 10-17:00.

The Old Man - *Damstraat 16, 627-0043*

This shop also rents skates for ƒ15 per day. ƒ250 deposit or credit card. Open mon-sat 09-18:00 (thurs 'til 21).

Silo Drome - *New Silo, Westerdoksdijk 51, 686-4322*

Cool new skating party once a week on thursday nights. (see Party Venues, Music section). Open 20-03:00. Entrance ƒ5. Skates for rent.

MOPEDS

Moped Rental Service Amsterdam - *Spuistraat 98, 422-0266*

Newly opened, just in time for the tourist season. The rental includes insurance and a full tank of gas. One hour ƒ12.50, second hour ƒ10, third hour ƒ7.50. Half day ƒ35, full day ƒ60.
Open daily 09-20:00.

PUBLIC TRANSPORT

Most people visiting Amsterdam stay mainly in the centre and don't have to rely too much on public transit. But if you need it, you'll find there's a good network of trams, buses and metro lines. The transit system operates largely on the honour system, so you can try to ride for free if you want, but if you get caught the "I'm a tourist; I didn't understand" routine usually won't work. The fine is ƒ60 plus the fare.

Amsterdam is divided into zones and the more zones you travel in the more expensive your ticket will be. If you'll be using public transit for more than one round trip your best bet is to buy a 15 strip "strippen kaart" for ƒ11. Most of central Amsterdam is one zone. For each ride in the centre you must stamp two strips on your card. You can do it yourself in one of the yellow boxes you'll find in most trams and metro stations, or you can ask the driver to do it. Your ticket is then valid for an hour within that zone (the last in the series of numbers stamped on your ticket is the time you embarked). You have to stamp an extra strip for each additional zone you want to travel. (One zone costs two strips. Two zones cost three strips, etc.) Buy these "strippen kaarten" at Central Station, post offices or tobacco shops.

Cultural imperialism hits the trams.

Single tickets can be purchased on trams and buses, but they're much more expensive, (ƒ3). To disembark your train, tram or bus push the button by the door. After midnight, night buses take over on most routes and the price goes up.

For more information and a free route map stop by the GVB (public transit) office. Walk across the little square in front of central station and you'll find it on your left, next to the VVV. They're open mon-fri 07-21:00, sat/sun 08-21:00. You can also call 06-92-92, but it costs ƒ.50 per minute.

TAXIS

Expensive, but if you really need one call 677-7777 and enjoy the service: taxis here are very comfortable. You can't flag one down on the street, but there are taxi stands at Central Station, Dam Square, Leidseplein, Rembrandtplein, Nieuwmarkt, the Tropenmuseum, etc.. Tipping isn't necessary, but of course if you want to the driver will be happy.

BOAT TOURS

Tours leave from several docks in front of central station and along the Damrak. It's very touristy, but I think it's fun to see the city from the canal perspective and some of the taped info is interesting. The tours usually give you a quick look at the harbour and then cruise along the canals while a recording in 4 languages describes the sights. The routes vary slightly, last one hour, depart every twenty minutes or so, and cost ƒ11. The canals are particularly beautiful at night. The last tours depart at 22:00 and are often sold out in advance.

Last year Reederij P. Kooij, just to the right when you come out of Central Station, had one hour tours for only ƒ5! They were exactly the same as the more expensive ones mentioned above and they left every 1/2 hour until 16:00. I hope they'll be back this year.

MOTOR BOATS

Aan de Wind Boat Rental
Across the street from the Amstel Hotel, 692-9124

Ahoy matey! This place rents four-seater rowboats with outboard motor at ƒ57.50 for 90 minutes. No deposit required, but you must leave a passport. Call to check on availability.

CANAL BIKES

Canal bikes, 2-4 person pedal bikes, are all over the old city canals in summer. Now ,I haven't actually gone on one, but it looks really fun and I think I'll try it this year. They can be rented at several locations including in front of the Rijksmuseum and Anne Frank House. Two persons ƒ19.50/hour; 4 person ƒ29.50/hour. Deposit ƒ50. Tel: 626-5574. Open in summer 09:30-22:30 daily. Spring and fall 10-17:00.

A NOTE ON BIKE THIEF MOTHERFUCKERS

Last year in Amsterdam over 150,000 bikes were stolen. Hot bikes are sold by sorry looking junkies who cruise around yelling "fiets te koop", but more bikes are actually stolen by organised gangs.

Junkies sell hot bikes very cheaply, but if you're tempted to buy one while you're here, think again. When you buy a stolen bike you're keeping the asshole who nicked it in business, and I don't want to lose my transportation because you want a cheap bike.

GETTING OUT OF AMSTERDAM

BUS

Eurolines, 627-5151

A lot of people assume that trains are the only alternative to cars for travel in Europe, but Eurolines has service to almost all major European cities and they are much cheaper than the train. However, not all routes are served daily and they often sell out in advance, so check it out early. Tickets can be purchased at Budget Bus (10 Rokin, near Dam Square), the International Lift Centre (see below) and many other travel agencies. If you have an International Student Identity Card there is a small discount.

Hoverspeed Ferry/Bus, 664-6626

This company has two departures daily to London. A return trip is ƒ160 (ƒ145 for students), making it a bit cheaper than Eurolines.

HITCHING

There is a lot of competition hitching out of Amsterdam in the summer, but people do give lifts. If you're heading to Utrecht, central or southern Germany take tram 25 to the end of the line and join the crowd on the Utrechtseweg. How about Groningen, northern Germany or Scandinavia? Hop the metro to Amstel station and try your luck on the Gooiseweg. For Leiden and The Hague go by tram 16 or 24 to Stadionplein and stick your thumb out at the Haarlemmerweg. Good luck.

I didn't tell you before, but I'm telling you now: hitching isn't allowed on the national motor way. Stay on the on-ramps or in gas stations. You'll avoid hassles from the cops and, anyway, it's easier for drivers to pick you up.

International Lift Centre - *Nieuwezijds Voorburgwal 256, 622-4342*

The Lift Centre serves as an intermediary between drivers and passengers looking for lifts. They are affiliated with Lift Centres all over Europe and should definitely be checked out as an alternative to the bus or train. To use the service you must become a member, which costs ƒ10 and is valid for one year. Note that this fee includes insurance - a good deal. If you have a car and want to take on passengers in order to cut costs call 622-4230. There is also a travel agency in the back specialising in budget tickets. Open mon-fri 10-18:00, sat 10-14:00.

TRAVELLERS' BULLETIN BOARD

The Tropenmuseum (see Museum section) has a bulletin board for travellers located near the entrance to the gift shop. If you're looking for a companion to travel with through other parts of the world this is a great source of information. There are also ads from people wanting to share driving to Africa and the Middle East.

AIR TRAVEL

The NBBS is the official Dutch student travel agency and is well worth checking out if you're looking for an air ticket. They have an office at Rokin 38 (just south of Dam Square). Take a number and be prepared to wait. This area has many travel agencies. My friend found a great deal to India at Cathay Travel (Oude Doelenstraat 3, 638-3684). Around the Nieuwmarkt, in Amsterdam's tiny Chinatown, are several agencies that are said to have some good deals to Asia. Shop around.

Airhitch (Aireka) - *Singel 302, 625-0909*

Listen-up for a cheap way to get to North America from Amsterdam. Holders of US or Canadian passports can buy stand-by tickets to several North American cities on chartered airlines. Prices start at US$169 to the east coast (Montreal, New York City), $229 to the south and midwest (Toronto, Chicago, Miami, Tampa, and Denver), $269 to the west coast (Vancouver, Seattle, LA, and San Francisco) to be paid in guilders. In return you receive a voucher that is fully refundable if you don't get on a flight after three attempts. This is a very good price for people with a bit of flexibility in their travel plans. Of course there are some restrictions, so go talk to the counsellors and ask what other destinations and departure cities they have as well. Open mon-fri 10-14:00, shorter hours in winter.

NS Travel Agency - *Schiphol Airport, 601-9494*

This branch office specialises in last minute charter tickets and packages throughout Europe and to North America. They sometimes have special deals with British Airways to anywhere that they fly. Give them a call. Open mon-fri 09:30-17:30, sat 09:30-14:30.

GETTING TO THE BEACH

Trains to Zandvoort (on the coast), leave approximately every half hour. On sunny days they are very crowded. The trip takes about half an hour and costs ƒ13.50 return. You can bring your bike for an extra charge. Zandvoort can get very crowded, the water isn't exactly clean, and it's often very windy. But the beach is big, wide and white, and a day trip there can be a lot of fun.

GETTING TO THE AIRPORT

Easy as pie! Hop on the train at Central Station (ƒ5.75) and you're there in about 20 minutes. Trains depart about every twenty minutes during the day from 06-23:30. Then 00:14. Then at 15 minutes to the hour every hour until 04:45. Then 05:03 and 05:31. (Did you know that Schiphol Airport is five metres below sea level?).

PRACTICAL SHIT

CHANGING MONEY

First of all, stay away from banks! They're all thieves and scum. That 1% surcharge you paid on your travellers cheques? Pure profit. They're already paid by the cheque companies to sell them! Then they've got the nerve to charge you commission when you cash them. Save your dough and go to a money-changer that doesn't charge commission. A good place that doesn't charge commission is the tourist shop at Damrak 17 to the right and across the street from the Grand Hotel Krasnapolsky. But places do change, so be sure to shop around.

The money-changers in the Leidseplein area are mostly a big rip-off: commission charges and low rates. Also beware of places that advertise no commission if you're purchasing (i.e. if you're buying US dollars). It's a scam and once they have your money inside their bullet-proof glass booth you won't get it back. (Checkpoint is notorious for pulling this one.)

The GWK in Central Station **is** a bank, but if you're stuck they're open all night.

PHONE

If you have to make a long distance call use the PTT Telehouse at Raadhuisstraat 46-50 (just west of the post office), which is operated by the Dutch phone company. The staff will dial for you and then hook you up to a line in your own little booth with a digital display of how much you're spending. The centre is open 24 hours a day.

Phone booths have instructions in English and you'll have to insert two 25 cent pieces. If you'll be making a lot of calls you may want to buy a phone-card which can be purchased in several denominations at the post office or tobacco shops, and are easy to use.

For long distance calls dial 00, then your country code and the number. Holland's country code is 31. Amsterdam's city code is 020.

Warning: avoid all the call centres on the tourist strips (like the Damrak). They're a rip-off and you'll end up spending big money.

POST OFFICE

monday-friday 09-18:00, saturday 10-13:30.

The main post office is at Singel 250 at the corner of Raadhuisstraat (just west of the Dam Square). Turn to your left inside the main entrance and take a number: no pushing, no shoving. The system here is very efficient and the people behind the counter speak English (like most Amsterdammers) and are really helpful. If you want special stamps go to the philatelic counter at your right as you enter the room. This is also a good way to avoid a long line at the "take a number" counters. A postcard anywhere overseas costs f.90 and letters up to 20 grams cost f1.60. Postcards in Europe cost f.70 and letters up to 20 grams, f.90. In the same room are telephones, a photocopier and a passport photo booth. I like this place.

The room to the right of the main entrance has a stationary store and a bank that changes money, but they're very slow and charge commission.

The entrance to the Poste Restante is down some stairs to the left of the main post office entrance. If you're having mail sent to you the address is: Poste Restante, Hoofdpostkantoor PTT, Singel 250, 1012 SJ, Amsterdam, The Netherlands. Don't forget to bring your passport when you go to pick up your letters. If you want to send or receive e-mail you can do it at Mystèr 2000 (see Party Venues, Music section).

FOOD

Eating out in Amsterdam is, on the whole, expensive. But if you listen to me and pay attention to this section I promise you a full belly at the best price.

If you're on the tightest budget, head to the markets for the cheapest fruit, veggies, cheese, etc. I've listed several in the shopping section. For dry goods go to the large supermarkets and remember to bring your own bags. If you are going to buy fruit and veggies at the supermarkets pick out what you want and put it on the scale. Push the button with the picture of what you're buying and the price appears. Then push the square marked "bon" and a sticker comes out for you to place on the bag. Some bad people then add a little more, but of course I would never advise you to do this.

SUPERMARKETS

Most are open mondays 13-18:00; tuesday, wednesday & fridays 09-18:00; thursdays 09-21:00; saturdays 09-17:00. Closed sundays and monday mornings.

Aldi - *Nieuwe Weteringstraat 26*

This is the cheapest, but they don't have as good a selection as the bigger chains.

Dagmarkt

Here are a couple of locations of this big west-side chain:

Elandsgracht 118 - In the Jordaan.
This street is really nice and this branch usually plays good music!
Rozengracht 193 - Also in the Jordaan.
For some reason the security guard here always follows me around.
Westerstraat 100 - Again in the Jordaan.
Across the street is an Albert Heijn supermarket.

Albert Heijn

This is a biggie in Amsterdam. Every time I blink there's a new one open.
Haarlemmerdijk 1 - A ten minute walk west of Central Station. This is also a nice street to explore.
Vijzelstraat 117 - At Kerkstraat.
Nieuwmarkt 18 - Just east of the Red Light District in the big square.
Waterlooplein 129-131 - At the Waterlooplein flea market.

HEALTH FOOD STORES

For a more complete guide to Amsterdam's health food stores, as well as restaurants and a map, pick up the little guide *Go For Good Food*. It's available at most health food stores for ƒ1.50.

De Aanzet - *Frans Hals Straat 27, 673-3415*

This is a pretty, co-operatively run store not far from the Albert Cuyp market. They stock some bulk products, organic fruits and veggies, and awesome baked goods. Open mon-fri 09-18:00, sat 09-17:00.

Gimsel - *Huidenstraat 19, 671-3505*

This store is located on a very nice street in the centre and it has a big bakery as well as all the other healthy stuff. Open mon-fri 08:30-18:00, sat 09-16:00.

Jakub Markus - *Nieuwe Kerkstraat 8, 625-1223*

You'll find this shop half a block from the famous old "skinny bridge" over the Amstel River. It's open mon 08:30-18:00, wed-fri 08:30-18:00, sat 08:30-16:00. Closed tues.

De Natuurwinkel - *Weteringschans 133, 638-4083*

Health food, supermarket style. Huge selection including produce, cheese, and bakery. Big, busy bulletin board. Open mon 10-18:00, tues-fri 09:00-18:00 (thurs 'til 21:00), sat 09:00-17:00.

TROPICAL SHOPS (Tropische Winkels)

These are fantastic little stores specialising in foods from tropical countries: everything from mangoes to hot sauce to black hair-care products. If you've got a place to do any cooking you should visit one for inspiration. They are found throughout the city, but here are a few of my favourites.

Tropica Sranang - *Haarlemmerdijk 17, 625-3443*

This "specialist in eastern products" (near the Prinsengracht) also has warm take-away Surinamese and Indonesian meals starting at ƒ7.50 for Gado-Gado. Open mon-fri 10-18:30, sat 10-17:00.

Tjin's Toko - *1e van der Helststraat 64, 671-7708*

Located right by the Albert Cuyp Market (see Markets, Shopping section). This store has all kinds of products including those hard to find tortillas. Open mon-fri 09:30-18:00, sat 09:30-17:00.

Tropische Winkel - *Dapperplein 9*

Smack-dab in the middle of the Dapper market (see Markets, Shopping section), you'll find this cheerful, music-filled shop. Good selection of tropical produce, canned goods and spicy take-away. Open mon-sat 09:00-18:00.

STREET FOODS

Scattered around the city are falafel & shoarma take-aways where prices start at ƒ4.50-ƒ5.50. For shoarma try the Damstraat (just east of Dam Square) where there's a whole row of these places. Make sure you specify "small" if that's what you want or they'll try to give you a large and embarrass you into paying for it. For the best deal on falafels go to **Maoz Falafel**, Reguliersbreestraat 41, (by Rembrandtplein). They give you the pita and falafel balls and you help yourself to the rest. All you can pile on for ƒ5. Burp!

For french fries (chips to you Brits) try any place that advertises "vlaamse frites" (Flemish fries). These are the best. There is a large choice of toppings, but get mayonnaise for the Dutch experience. There's one on Damrak between the Dam and Central Station. There's also a good one on the Korte Leidsedwarsstraat north of Leidsestraat (near Leidseplein), and maybe the best of all is Voetboogstraat 33 (which runs parallel to the Kalverstraat). A small is usually ƒ2-ƒ2.50, plus ƒ.50 for a big selection of sauces. Delicious.

Fish lovers should definitely try snacking at one of the herring stalls that are all over the city. They're easily recognisable by their fish flags. All kinds of fish and seafood sandwiches are available from ƒ2.75. There is one close to Central Station on the bridge where the Haarlemmerstraat crosses the Singel canal.

Another good bet for cheap food is Indonesian or Surinamese take away. A big roti meal is about ƒ6-ƒ7. A large plate of fried rice with chicken and pork runs about ƒ9-ƒ10 and is often enough for two people. These places are all over town. At Rozengracht 5 near the Westerkerk is a good place called Aurora (open sunday to friday 16-22:00; closed saturday). Near the Albert Cuyp Market (at 1st Van Der Helststraat 55) is an excellent, eat-in and take-away place called Warung Marlin. Big servings here cost ƒ7-ƒ12 and they play great soul music. (But for the best deal see Restaurants, this section).

For cheap Chinese take away look around Nieuwmarkt where there's a small Chinatown. And at the markets don't forget to try the cheap and addictive Vietnamese Loempias (spring rolls); veggie or meat, ƒ1.

Febo is the name of a chain of gross automats that you'll see all over the city. Here you can get greasy, deep-fried snacks for a guilder or two. In my opinion, your best bet is the kaas (cheese) soufflé. Here are a few locations: Damrak 6 (just down from Central Station); Kalverstraat 142; Nieuwendijk 220. They're open every night 'til 03:00.

The sandwich shop downstairs in the metro stop at Central Station (take the stairs by the VVV) often has potato salad sandwiches on special for only $f1$!

NIGHT SHOPS

These small "convenience" stores are the only places to buy groceries after 18:00 and are accordingly expensive. Fruit and veggies at these shops are a rip-off, but all the usual junk foods are available. Most night shops are open daily from 16-01:00. Here are a few in the centre.

Pinguin Nightshop - *Berenstraat 5. Between the Prinsengracht and the Keizersgracht.*

Big Bananas - *Leidsestraat 73. This night shop does a lot of business because of its location, but what a grumpy bunch.*

Avondmarkt - *de Wittenkade 94-96. West end. The best selection and prices.*

Sterk - *Waterlooplein 241*

Baltus T - *Vijzelstraat 127*

Texaco - *Sarphatistraat 225. Open 24 hours. Eat here and get gas.*

ALL NIGHT EATING

Dalia Snackbar - *Oude Hoogstraat 21*
All kinds of cheap meals are available here 'til late at night. Open weekdays until 03:00, weekends 'til 04:00.

Bojo - *Lange Leidsedwarsstraat 51*
This Indonesian restaurant (see Restaurants in this section) is open saturday and sunday until 06:00 and weeknights until 02:00. It's a good place for a late night pig-out.

Febo Snackbars - *all over*
I can't really recommend this shit, but they're open late and they're cheap (see Street Food in this section). Do what you gotta do.

New York Pizza - *Leidsestraat 23*
Pizza slices available until 3 am on fridays and saturdays.

Baklava Shop - Wen Shou Lin - *Heisteeg 5, 638-8438*
This little Turkish shop is owned by a very friendly Chinese woman. You can buy Turkish bread, Chinese buns and other treats. Located just off Spui circle. Open mon-thurs 10-01:00, fri-sun 10-03:00.

SUNDAYS

Baklava Shop - Wen Shou Lin - *Heisteeg 5, 638-8438*
Open for munchies on sunday, (see above).

Outmayer Bakeries - *24 Reguliersbreestraat/Damrak, 59/Nieuwendijk 227A, 622-4674*
Fresh bread and pastries.

Delifrance - *Reguliersbreestraat 25, 624-0200*
Breads and sandwiches.

FREE SAMPLES

I don't know how desperate you are but...

In the departure lounge at Schiphol airport there are two deli-style shops that serve samples of cheeses and sausages. Delicious! Marks and Spencer (Kalverstraat 66) is in a big shopping area. The other day in the food section (rear main floor) I found a tray of smoked salmon, and some expensive Belgian chocolate! Unfortunately they don't put out samples every day, but when they do it's a good opportunity to sample traditional yuppie cuisine. Gary's Muffins, at Marnixstraat 121 (see Cafés), almost always has one or two baskets on the counter with samples of his goodies. Don't expect to get out of here without buying something though: there are too many good things to try.

BREAKFAST

Breakfast is such a good meal, but if you're travelling on a budget you don't want to be forking out a lot of dough, especially so early in the day. If you can't find a hotel that includes breakfast, (see Hotels, Places to Sleep section), then here is a selection of eating spots where you can get something for less than ƒ10. Most of the these places also have traditional English or American breakfasts, but not for under ƒ12-15.

For the record, an Uitsmijter (pronounced outsmyter), means bouncer, and it's what you serve your guests late at night just before you kick them out of your flat. It consists of an egg fried with cheese, ham or another meat and slipped onto a piece of toast. It's very Dutch.

Finally, before you order coffee please read the introduction to the Cafés section in this book. It might save your life (or at least ƒ2.50).

Barney's Breakfast Bar - *Haarlemmerstraat 102, 625-9761 (1)*

Psssst. This is also a coffeeshop so you can get stoned while you munch. Muesli and yoghurt ƒ5. Fruit and yoghurt ƒ5.50. Scrambled eggs on toast ƒ7. Uitsmijters from ƒ8. Nice coffee in a big cup. Pleasant atmosphere, english happily spoken, and located on an interesting shopping street. B-fast served all day. Open daily 09:30-19:30.

Café Mono - *Oudezijds Voorburgwal 2, 625-3630 (2)*

Located at the edge of the Red Light District. Cornflakes or muesli with yoghurt ƒ5.25. Mushroom omelette and toast ƒ6. Fresh squeezed orange juice ƒ3. Good music! (See Cafés section for details). B-fast served daily until 06:00. Open sun-thurs 10-01:00, fri,sat 10-02:00.

Winkel Lunchcafé - *Noordermarkt 43, 623-0223 (3)*

If you're visiting one of the markets by the Noorderkerk on saturday or monday morning (see Markets, Shopping section) be sure to stop in at this very popular café on the corner of the square. They have one of the best apple cakes in Amsterdam. Everyone gets a piece and sits outside drinking cappuccino or fresh orange juice at shared tables along the crowded Westerstraat. You'll be stuffed after one slice. Open mon-sat 07-18:00.

RESTAURANTS

Albert Cuyp 67 - *Albert Cuyp 67, 671-1396 (4)*

Surinamese and Chinese. What a deal! This little restaurant lies between two others that have basically the same menu, but this was the first one I tried, so I usually go here. Big portions for a low price. Try the "roti kip" (curried chicken, potatoes, cabbage, egg, and a roti) for only ƒ5! There are plenty of choices for vegetarians too. Meals run from ƒ5-ƒ12,50 and don't be shy to ask what's what. Excellent banana chips. Located near Albert Cuyp Market. Open mon-sat 10-22:00, sun 12-22:00.

Friendship Hotel - *Van Eeghenstraat 22, 662-1828 (5)*

Vegetarian. This hotel has been taken over by a bunch of squatters who've

Restaurants

turned the basement into the best squat restaurant in Amsterdam. The chef is incredible! Six nights a week he cooks up a huge, nutritionally balanced meal for only ƒ7.50. A recent menu: an appetiser of deep-fried hemp seed veggie snacks with sauce and a salad; a main course consisting of a bean-filled empanada, greens, brown rice with vegetables, eggplant parmesan; dessert of chocolate mousse with fruit. Beer starts at ƒ2 a bottle and juice is ƒ1. The atmosphere is very relaxed, friendly, and full of different languages. Make an effort to get here; you won't be disappointed. It's located very close to Vondelpark. To get in, bang at the basement window to the right of the door. Open daily. Dinner served at 20:00.

Restaurant Susy Cream Cheese - *Cliffordstraat 36, 682-0411*

Vegetarian. Every friday night this community centre serves up a fantastic three course meal from a different country. The place is plant-filled and cosy, buzzing with conversation and soft jazz. The appetiser costs ƒ2.50, the main course ƒ7.50, and dessert ƒ2.50, making a complete meal ƒ12,50, but you don't have to order every course (of course). And a bottle of Grolsch

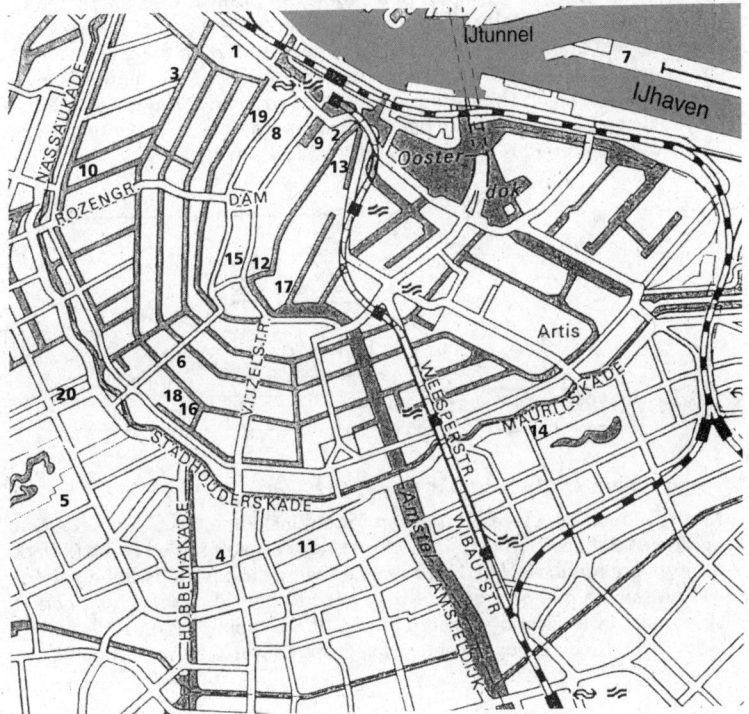

beer is only ƒ1.75! Call 684-4865 for a reservation or show up early. Bus 18 or tram 10 from Central Station. Open friday 18-20:30.

Westermarkt Squat - *Westermarkt 7, 420-6267 (6)*

Vegetarian/Vegan. Let's hope these people never get evicted because they have a fantastic cook! Complete meals are served two nights a week for only ƒ5! Tuesday night is vegan food and wednesday is vegetarian. The place is small and a bit grungy and crowded: there's room for about 25 people and their dogs. Add to that some Suicidal Tendencies on the stereo and you have the makings of an interesting evening. Right across the street is the Westerkerk (west church). Call for a reservation. Open tues and wed 19:00.

Einde van de Wereld - *Sumatrakade 15 (7)*

Home-cooked. This eleven year old squat restaurant really looks like it's at the end of the world until you step inside to bright lights, great music and some terrific food. Go early as they only serve until the food runs out, and it always does. There's a choice of a vegetarian or meat dish for ƒ8-ƒ12 or a half serving (lots of kids here) for about ƒ6. It's a great deal: the servings are huge and there's also fresh bread and garlic butter on the tables. Drinks are cheap. Order, leave your name, pay, and in about 15 minutes they'll bring you your meal. This restaurant is a bit hard to find. You can take a bus or you'll need a bike. If you're here for any length of time, make the effort. Einde van de Wereld is open wed and fri only, from 18:00.

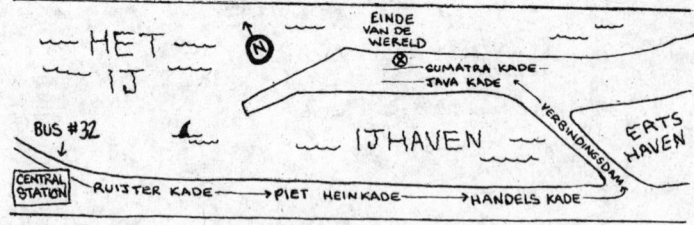

The Egg Cream - *St Jacobsstraat 19, 623-0575 (8)*

Mostly vegetarian. I took a lot of shit for not including this place in the first edition of Get Lost!, so here it is. Mostly veggie meals served in a laid-back atmosphere for about ƒ14. I recommend their delicious soups. Set menu for ƒ17 gets you a pile of food, but they need to get rid of that supermarket sliced bread. No alcohol. Located in one of the rapidly disappearing alleyways off of Nieuwezijds Voorburgwal. Open daily except tues 11-20:00.

Restaurants

Kam Yin - *Warmoesstraat 6, 625-3115 (9)*

Surinamese/Chinese. The best food of this type at a good price in the centre of Amsterdam. They have a big menu of rice and noodle dishes and the servings are huge. Prices start at about ƒ8.50 and one dish along with a side order is probably enough for two people. Two minutes from Central Station. Open daily 13-24:00.

Vliegende Schotel (Flying Saucer) - *Nieuwe Leliestraat 162, 625-2041 (10)*

Vegetarian. This restaurant is situated in a beautiful neighbourhood called the Jordaan (pronounced yordahn), so make sure that you take a walk around before or after your meal. They have a big menu that includes some vegan dishes. Soup of the day for ƒ3.50. Meals start at ƒ11.00, and half-servings from ƒ7.50. Comfy and friendly. Open daily 17:30-23:30, but meals are only served from 17:30-22:15.

De Malle Monkey - *Govert Flinckstraat 193 (11)*

Vegetarian. This is one of Amsterdam's coolest new squat restaurants. Three times a week they serve a big plate of veggie food for only ƒ6.50. The menu changes each night, but fridays are always Mexican. Beer or fresh squeezed juice is ƒ2. The atmosphere is very laid-back, grungy, and welcoming. It's a mellow space for hanging out and having a smoke before or after your meal. The bar is always open. The building used to house a gym and in keeping with this theme the squat is open every day for shooting hoops or playing table tennis. Monday night has become juggling night and look out for funk jams happening sunday afternoons. The entrance is through the red door on the right side of the building. Buzz to get in. Meals served mon/wed/fri from 20:00.

Pannekoekhuis Upstairs - *Grimburgwal 2, 626-5603 (12)*

Pancakes. Not having a pancake in Holland would be like coming here and not seeing a windmill. It's part of the Dutch experience. This tiny place is on the second floor of an old house and it's very cosy. They have an english menu with prices starting at about ƒ6 for a powdered sugar topping. A pancake with strawberries and whipped cream goes for ƒ10.50. Students get a 10% discount. Open tues-sun 12-19:00.

The Graan Silo - *Westerdoksdijk 51 (last door on your right at the far end of the building)*

Vegetarian. The Graan Silo (grain silo) is a fantastic squat on the western docklands. About 35 artists are living in this giant old building and up to 70 other artists are also using the space for all kinds of work and performances. One of their projects is a very cool restaurant in one corner of the building. Come early (at about 18:00) to place your order, as they can only accommodate a certain number of people. Then relax and have a cheap drink while your food is prepared. Meals are very inexpensive (about ƒ7) and they cook all kinds of veggie dishes from thick soups with homebaked bread to sushi. At about 20:00 the meal is served. The restaurant has big windows overlooking the water and the space has a slightly twisted medieval look to it with candles and sculptures casting shadows on the stone walls. Open for dinner every tues, fri and sun. Go.

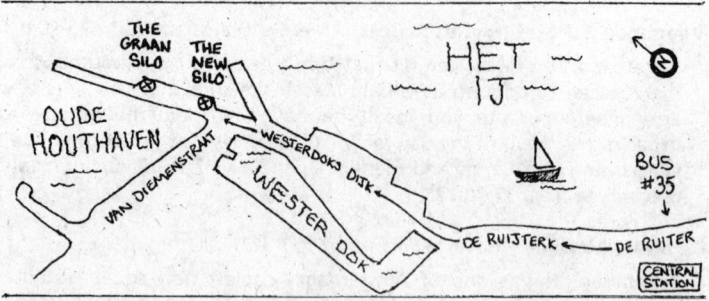

New York Pizza - *Reguliersbreestraat 17, Leidsestraat 23, Spui 2, 420-3538*

Pizza. I'm not usually into fast food chains, but in a city that doesn't know how to make pizza these are damn good slices. Prices run from ƒ3.45-ƒ4.75. There are only a few seats inside the Spui location, but if the weather is good turn right out the door and walk one block until you see a small arched doorway on your right. The beautiful courtyard you'll find inside is called the Begijnhof. Spui location open mon 11:30-22:00, tues, wed 11-22:00, thurs-sat 11-24:00, sun 11-21:00. Leidsestraat open sun-thurs 10-01:00, fri/sat 10-03:00.

Thaise Snackbar Bird - *Zeedijk 77, 420-6289 (13)*

Thai. If you've ever been to Thailand you'll like this place. It's got the atmosphere down pat, with Thai pop songs, pictures of the king, and orchids on the tables. A lot of Thai people eat here, which is a good sign of authentic cooking. Meals aren't super cheap (average ƒ14), but the food is always prepared fresh and it's delicious. Worth the walk through this sleazy, junkie filled neighbourhood. Open daily 13-20:00, but closed wed.

Sleepin Restaurant - *'s-Gravesandestraat 51, 694-7444 (14)*

Everything. The restaurant at this famous hostel/hotel (see Places to Sleep section), isn't really exciting, but the food is good and reasonably priced. The menu changes regularly and usually consists of a couple of meat and potato dishes as well as something vegetarian, with an average price of ƒ12. They play all types of music, have candles on the tables, and I find the atmosphere mellow and comfortable. Don't go out of your way, but if you're staying in the area or if you're going to see a concert here you might want to give it a try. Nice terrace in the summer. Open daily 18-22:30.

La Place Grand Café Restaurant - *Kalverstraat 201, 622-0171 (15)*

Everything. This is a department store food court, but without the usual fast-food crap. Elegant little booths display a wide variety of beautiful fresh fruits and vegetables bought directly from the producers. They also claim that most of their meat is free-range. The menu changes daily and everything is prepared fresh. When you enter you'll be given a card. Don't lose it, or you'll be fined ƒ100! As you create your meal with things from different stalls, the price is stamped on your card. You pay when you leave. Some examples from the last time I ate here: 1/2 chicken and chips ƒ6.95 (other meat dishes ƒ10-15). Sandwiches ƒ4-5. Liqueur coffees ƒ5. It's a good place to seek refuge from the crowds of the Kalverstraat and they actually have a non-smoking section. Open daily 09-22:00.

Rimini - *Lange Leidsedwarsstraat 75, 622 7014 (16)*

Italian. This restaurant advertises all pizzas and pastas for "half price plus 1 guilder". The cheapest pizza is a thin but big margherita for ƒ5.50, which means you can have a pizza and a beer for about ƒ8.00: a good deal.

The Atrium - *Oudezijds Achterburgwal 237 (17)*

Cafetaria food. This is a self-service student mensa with cheap meals (even cheaper for students) from about ƒ6-ƒ8. Off-meal times it's also a pleasant place to grab an inexpensive cup of coffee and a croissant and to rest your feet a bit. Meals are served mon-fri 12-14:00 and 17-19:00. There's another student mensa, (Agora, Roetersstraat 13), that also has cheap meals and a big non-smoking section. Same hours as the Atrium.

Bojo - *Lange Leidsedwarsstraat 51, 622-7434 (18)*

Indonesian. This place is in all the tourist guides, but a lot of Dutch people go here too because the servings are huge and the prices are reasonable (ƒ13-ƒ18). Skip the appetisers, they're not very good. They also have a stupid rule that if you sit outside they won't give you a glass of water. Open sun-thurs 17-02:00 and fri/sat until 06:00. The food is pretty good here, but if you want a real Indonesian rice table (and they're excellent) you have to pay about ƒ30.00 per person. If you have the dough try "Cilubang" (Runstraat 10) where the food is fantastic.

Keuken van 1870 - *Spuistraat 4, 624 8965 (19)*

Cafetaria food. It opened as a soup kitchen in 1870, and you can still get a very cheap meal here. Full course meat and potato dishes go for ƒ10. It's close to Central Station. Open mon-fri 11:30-20:00 and sat 16-21:00.

Restaurant Hap Hmm - *1st Helmerstraat 33, 618-1884 (20)*
Dutch food. Just like dinner in mom's kitchen. Hap Hmm is located on a street running parallel to the Overtoom. For ƒ10.75 you get soup, potatoes, veggies and a meat dish. Dessert is another ƒ1.25. It's nothing fancy, but it's a good price for a filling Dutch meal in a homey environment. Open sun-fri 16-19:30.

A NOTE ABOUT SQUATTING IN AMSTERDAM

If a building in Amsterdam remains empty for more than a year without the owner putting it to some use, it can be squatted. This law is meant to protect the city from speculators who sit on their property while prices rise due to the severe housing shortage.

That doesn't mean that squatters have an easy time taking over a building. The legal definition of occupancy is a slippery one, and new legislation is making it increasingly difficult to have a building defined as vacant. In addition, a great deal of work is usually needed to make a squat habitable and often legal battles ensue.

I have a lot of respect for those who have chosen to live as squatters as an expression of their political beliefs. They are simultaneously working to preserve and create housing in this overcrowded city. Several of these organised squats have opened restaurants and clubs that are some of the best in Amsterdam. Many of them live under imminent threat of being forced out by banks and developers. Going to these squats is a way of showing your support for a creative, co-operative way of living as well as your opposition to conservative pigs who care more about money than people.

For a fascinating historical and political (though slightly dated) perspective on the city's squats, pick up a copy of the booklet "This Is Not A Tour Guide" (ƒ5). It takes the form of a walking tour. For a copy call SPOK (620-6826), a 15 year old organisation run by volunteers, that provides active support to tenants and squatters.

CAFÉS

Amsterdam's cafés are plentiful and great places for hanging out and getting a feel for the city. Once you've ordered you'll be left alone to read or write postcards or vegetate for as long as you like. Don't be shy to ask to share a table if you see a free chair: this is one of the most densely populated countries in the world and table sharing is customary.

"Koffie verkeerd" (literally "incorrect coffee") is café au lait and if you order "ordinary coffee" you'll probably get an espresso. Tea is charged by the cup and extra water will be added to your bill. I don't know the reason for this dumb custom.

Many cafés also serve snacks such as broodjes (small sandwiches) and tostis (usually ham and cheese sandwiches squashed into a sandwich toaster). Prices start at about ƒ2.50 for a plain cheese-on-white-roll or tosti. Another popular item is incredible apple cake with whipped cream. It's an Amsterdam speciality that should definitely be experienced.

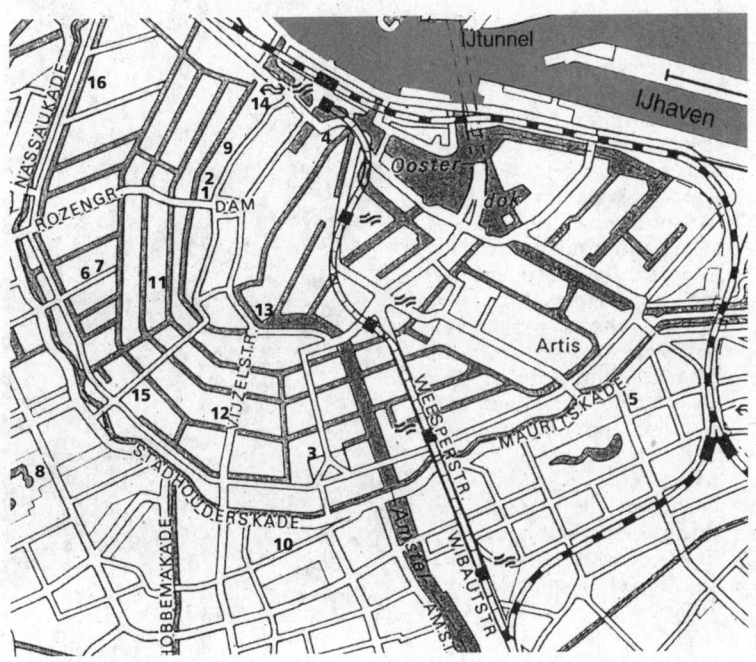

Villa Zeezicht - *Torensteeg 7 (1)*

Even with their recent expansion into the shop next door, this is a cosy café. The seats by the big windows are perfect for reading the paper and people-watching. In the summer there are tables outside and on the bridge. They make an awesome apple cake for ƒ4.50 (a meal in itself). Make sure to ask for whipped cream. Open mon-fri 8-18:30, sat and sun 9-18:30.

Café ter Kuile - *Singel 159 (2)*

This pretty café/bar gets very crowded in the day with students from the university. But at night after the dinner hour it becomes mellower. I'm talking candles on the table, Tom Waits on the stereo, and a good buzz of conversation. It's a good place to shoot the shit with a friend. Open daily 11-01:00, fri and sat 'til 02:00.

Backstage Boutique and Coffee-Corner
Utrechtsedwarsstraat 67, 622-3638 (3)

At first I thought I was in Pee Wee Herman's café, but a quick look at the photos adorning the "ego wall" set me straight. This is definitely the home of Greg and Gary, the Christmas Twins. These identical twins used to be big stars back in the US And they were wearing Travis Bickle mohawks when Scorsese was still in little school! This place is great! They serve coffees, teas, juices and an assortment of sandwiches and cakes. The bottom of the menu proclaims "Mama wanted girls!" The walls are decorated with wild sweaters and hats that are designed and made by the twins, who, if you're nice, might give you a postcard of themselves. These guys are super friendly and very funny. They're open mon-sat 10-18:00.

The "ego wall".

Cafés

Café Mono - *Oudezijds Voorburgwal 2, 625-3630 (4)*

Unfortunately I can't hang out at this hip café/bar because I'm allergic to the black and white cats (who happen to match the decor). But in nice weather they have tables out front along the canal. They specialise in breakfasts and alcohol, the former being served until 18:00, and often the twain shall meet. A mushroom omelette and toast is ƒ6. A giant breakfast with everything that entails is ƒ12,50. Music runs the course of garage, sixties, and some punk. Every thursday night there is a d.j. for their "wild sixties surf special", and fridays and saturdays often see live bands. Café Mono is located at the edge of the red light district, not far from Central Station. Open sun-thurs 10-01:00, fri/sat 10-02:00.

East of Eden - *Linnaeusstraat 11A, 665-0743 (5)*

A spacious café right across the street from the Tropenmuseum (see Museum section). The seating is a mish-mash of couches and easy chairs and lots of light comes in through high windows on two sides. It's warm and mellow and the only problem is that it gets very smoky. Non-smokers should visit this café in the summer when they have an outdoor terrace. Open daily 11-01:00.

Café Saarein - *Elandsstraat 119, 623-4901 (6)*

I wandered into this bar without knowing it was a women only café and I left as soon as I realised (o.k. I was actually asked to leave), but I was there long enough to see that it's a very cool place. True to its traditional "brown café" decor, the atmosphere is lively and all kinds of women come here to hang out and have a drink. There's a billiard table downstairs, magazines, and a shelf full of flyers too. Open mon 20- 01:00, tues-thurs 15-01:00, fri-sun 15-02:00.

COC - *Rozenstraat 14, 626-3087 (7)*

This café is in the home of Amsterdam's main gay and lesbian resource centre. Its relaxed atmosphere and considerate staff make this a good spot to have a drink and find out about gay happenings in Amsterdam. Look for a copy of *Out on the Streets* or *Rainbow Magazine*. Both are free, have some english articles and listings of gay events. The Queer Cult Parties take place here and sound like fun. Friday nights they host a mixed dance and there's a women-only dance every saturday night. Doors open at 22:00 and admission is only ƒ5. The café is open wed-sat 13-17:00.

Café Vertigo - *Vondelpark 3, 589-1400 (8)*

This place has one of the nicest terraces in Amsterdam. It's located in the middle of Vondelpark in the Film Museum building (see Film section). In bad weather duck into the cosy, low ceilinged café where on sunday afternoons you can often hear live jazz. Sometimes there are slide shows in the back. Note the cool sculpture that changes colour. Open daily 11-01:00.

Greenwoods - *Singel 103, 623-7071 (9)*

An Australian opened this café almost 7 years ago and despite the fact that it's trendy right now I still like it. It gets very crowded around lunch, but at other times it's a calm place to have some tea and a bite to eat. There aren't many places in A'dam where you can get a pot of tea (ƒ4.50). They also have bagels with cream cheese, tomato and lettuce (ƒ4.50), and selection of homebaked cakes and scones. Open mon-fri 09:30-19:00, sat,sun 11-19:00.

De Badcuyp - *1e Sweelinckstraat 10, 675-9669 (10)*

This former bathhouse was saved from demolition by activists in the neighbourhood. Now it's a "centre for art, culture and politics" that's run by volunteers. It's located in the middle of the crowded Albert Cuyp Market (see Markets, Shopping section), and in nice weather there are tables outside. Inside it's spacious and relaxed: newspapers are scattered around and art exhibits line the walls. The upper level gives you a good view of everyone shopping in the market below. They have a bar that serves snacks and full meals. Most nights there is live music, either in the café or in the hall upstairs. Open tues-thurs 11-01:00, fri,sat 11-02:00, sun 11-01:00.

Café de Pels - *Huidenstraat 25, 622-9037 (11)*

Traditional "brown" café with a diverse clientele. Warm and welcoming in the winter, while in the summer tiny outdoor tables make for good people watching on this quaint little street. It has a real Amsterdam ambiance. Open daily 13-01:00.

Françoise - *Kerkstraat 176, 624-0145 (12)*

This big café has a relaxed lived-in feel to it: plants, wood tables, and classical music make it a comfortable space to lounge awhile and write a letter. It's a lesbian hangout, but draws a mixed crowd. Meals and snacks available. No alcohol. Also changing art exhibits. Open mon-sat 09-18:00.

De Jaren - *Nieuwe Doelenstraat 20, 625-5771 (13)*

I find the food overpriced here, but I like the spaciousness, which is unusual for this city and means that you can always find a seat. In the summer there are two big terraces with a view over the Amstel River. Lots of intellectuals hang out reading books. I often stop in to use the toilet. Located between Waterlooplein and Rembrandtplein. Open sun-thurs 10-01:00, fri, sat 10-02:00.

Oibibio - *Prins Hendrikkade 20-21, 553-9355 (14)*

What makes this café special is it's spectacular interior, recently and beautifully renovated. Much of it has been restored to it's original 1883 splendour. The rest of the building houses a new-age cultural centre that includes a gorgeous sauna. Explore a bit if you have time. Directly opposite Central Station. Open sun-thurs 10-01:00, fri/sat 10-02:00.

Gary's Muffins - *Prinsengracht 454, 420-1452 (15)*
Marnixstraat 121, 638-0186 (16)

Muffin's, brownies, chewy chocolate chip cookies and yes, bagels. Don't get too excited if you're used to Montreal or New York bagels, (the owner of this place is from LA). But if you haven't had one in a while they're pretty good. Go for the bagel with cream cheese for ƒ3.25. The Prinsengracht location, which is just off Leidsestraat, is the location I like better in nice weather because of the tables out by the canal. Otherwise I go to the Marnixstaat shop which is airier and more comfortable inside. It also often has day-olds for ƒ1. Open mon-sat 08-18:00.

CANNABIS

If you like to smoke marijuana and hash, and come from anywhere other than the Parvati Valley, then you're in for a treat. In Amsterdam you can walk into any one of dozens of "coffeeshops" (cafés selling hash and grass), and order a coffee and a joint; then sit back and smoke, listen to music, perhaps have a game of backgammon or chess, without the worry of being arrested. How civilised!

To find coffeeshops look for places with cool names or trippy paint jobs, pictures of Bob Marley or lots of plants in the windows. A lot of coffeeshops now have a standard sign with big red lips smoking a joint. It doesn't get more obvious than that.

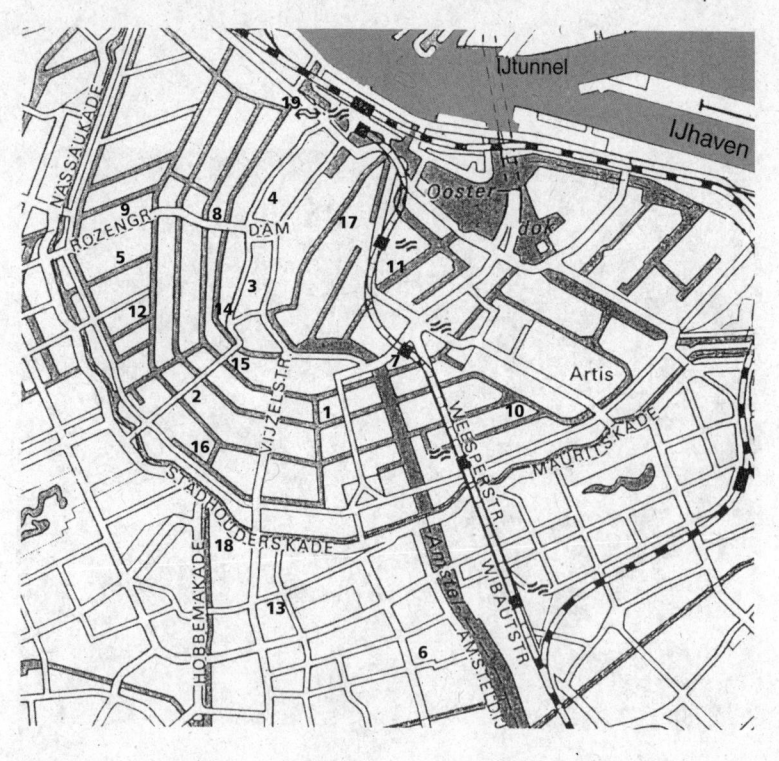

The most recent and comprehensive guide to coffeeshops is the *Dutch Hash Coffeeshop Tour* by Anonymous. I haven't seen *The Kind Guide* yet, but it sounds interesting with a map and descriptions of over 30 coffeeshops for ƒ2.50. Everything else on the market now is just pay-to-be-in-it tourist crap. Those of you interested in marijuana culture might want to pick up a copy of *Soft Secrets*, a newspaper all about growing and smoking in Holland. It features a mixture of Dutch and English articles, and at ƒ1 it makes a great gift for collectors back home. Also worth grabbing is *Highlife*, another Dutch cannabis culture magazine. It's more glossy and sells for ƒ4 in most coffeeshops and drug paraphernalia stores.

Your average coffeeshop has an alcohol-free bar, a few tables and chairs, maybe some couches, a pinball or slot machine, sometimes a fusball or pool table, and several board games. It's a standard formula that also includes a menu of tea, coffee, juice and a few snacks. What sets some coffeeshops apart from others is the decor and atmosphere, which is important when you're smoking.

Almost all coffeeshops have a menu listing the types of smoke available and where they're from. Its a lot of fun to try grass from different parts of the world, but I have to say that a lot of the Nederwiet (Dutch grown weed, such as Skunk and Northern Lights) is spectacular. Prices are listed by the gram and almost always sold in ƒ10 or ƒ25 bags. So if, for instance, Thai weed is selling for ƒ12 a gram, a ƒ10 bag will contain 0.8 grams. Don't be shy to ask to see the menu, it's there to make it easy for you. If there is no menu then an in-house dealer will make themselves known to you and happily explain what's available. Then relax while you roll and ponder the absurdity of North America's repressive and hypocritical "war on drugs", and how fantastic it is to be in Amsterdam!

Attention: don't buy anything on the street! You will definitely be ripped off!

Warning: Space Cakes and bon bons (containing grass or hash) are sold in some coffee shops. They can be very strong, almost like tripping, so have fun, but be prepared for a long, intense high. Also keep in mind that they can take up to a couple of hours to kick in, so don't gobble down another one just because you don't feel anything right away............ What?

COFFEESHOPS

Lucky Mothers - *Keizersgracht 665, 622-9617 (1)*
One of my favourites, this small, cosy coffeeshop is in a beautiful old canal house not far from Rembrantplein. In the afternoon sunlight spills in, making it an inviting place to sip fresh orange juice and read some of the newspapers and magazines lying about. They serve all kinds of delicious, healthy food (including hempburgers ƒ5), and they even have three types of organically grown buds. Friendly staff and lots of plants and artwork. Open sun-fri 09:30-20:00, sat 09:30-21:00.

Global Chillage - *Kerkstraat 51, 639-1154 (2)*

Most nights find the pillows and couches lining this "chill out lounge" full of stoned, happy people. The lighting, decor, and ambient music all work to create an atmosphere of, well... global chillage! Hopefully this is the beginning of a new wave of coffeeshops that will offer more than just a place to smoke and hang out, but that are also works of art in themselves. Anyway, this is the coolest new coffeeshop in Amsterdam and it's fitting that it should open along the trendy strip of Kerkstraat just off Leidsestraat. Open daily 11-24:00.

Kadinsky - *Rosmarijnsteeg 9, 624-7023 (3)*

A hip coffeeshop with an area upstairs that's perfect for kicking back and smoking that first joint of the evening. The music is usually in the acid jazz groove, but it depends on who's working. Tasty chocolate chip cookies also available. Open sun-thurs 10-01:00, fri/sat 12-02:00.

Homegrown Fantasy - *Nieuwezijds Voorburgwal 87a, 627-5683 (4)*

This is a better known coffeeshop, especially since it won the 1992 Cannabis Cup Award. It's also the home of the Dutch Passion seed company (see Seed Co.s, below). They have a large, tasty selection of Dutch grown grass and a couple of types of hash. Homegrown recently underwent a big renovation and I have to admit that I kind of miss the old colour scheme, but it's still got a fun, laid-back atmosphere. I like it here best in the daytime when the light is nice and time just seems to slow... right....... down. The black light in the toilet makes your teeth glow and your pee look like milk! Open daily 12-23:00.

Kunst And Koffie - *2nd Laurierdwarsstraat 64, 622-5960 (5)*

A really nice coffeeshop/gallery in the Jordaan with big windows and lots of local art. Buy your smoke in the basement where they often weigh it out for you. The room upstairs in the back has a couple of video games and lots of backgammon sets. Their snack menu includes muesli with yoghurt and chocolate chip cookies. It's a funky place - an artists' hang out. Open mon to sat 10-20:00.

Greenhouse - *Tolstraat 91, 673-7430 (6)*

These guys were big winners at the 7th Cannabis Cup Awards. Their excellent Cytral Skunk buds took first place in the Bio category and second overall. They also took first and second place in the Imported category. In addition, this location won the cup for best coffeeshop in Amsterdam. A lot of effort has gone into the design of this shop and you should take time to admire the cool mosaics and other decor. Upstairs are a couple of pool tables where they have regular tournaments. Even though it's a bit out of the centre it's worth the trek, but if you really can't make it check out their sister shop which just opened this spring (see below). Open sun-thurs 10-01:00, fri/sat 10-02:00.

Greenhouse - *Waterlooplein 345, 622-5499 (7)*

The owner of this brand new Greenhouse has done a fantastic job of turning what could have been just another coffeeshop into a work of art. The toilets alone took three months to complete! I recently spent a very relaxing afternoon here sitting at a candle-lit table, listening to music, and looking out the big window. As far as smokables go, Greenhouse took a place in almost every category of the 1994 Cannabis Cup, so indulge. They are also the only coffeeshops where you can taste the incredible White Butterfly (a.k.a. White Widow). Open sun-thurs 09-01:00, fri/sat 09-02:00.

A NOTE ON DRUGS IN AMSTERDAM

Once again Holland leads the western world in progressive thinking and action: soft drugs like cannabis and hashish have been decriminalised for over 15 years. Small amounts of these harmless substances can be bought, sold, and consumed without interference by the police.

Trafficking in hard drugs is dealt with seriously, but addiction is considered a matter of health and social well-being rather than a criminal/law enforcement problem. The number of addicts in Holland, where they can receive treatment without fear of criminal prosecution, is much lower than other countries where the law is used to strip people of their human rights (not to mention their property).

Some member states of the European Union are putting pressure on Holland to conform to their repressive drug policies. This has resulted in the threat of mass coffeeshop closures and proposals of more restrictions on cannabis trade. Retailers and consumers think this is bullshit. Don't let it happen. Speak out!

Dude with a bong..

The Grey Area - *Oude Leliestraat 2, 420-4301 (8)*

Originally this coffeeshop was also Amsterdam's first hempseed restaurant. Now they only serve tasty morsels of the smokable kind. They have a very select menu offering some of the newest strains of weed around, as well as some hash, and prices reflect this exclusivity. But connoisseurs will definitely get a kick out of this place. The little old house it's in and the street it's on are both exceptionally beautiful. Open wed-sat 12-22:00, sun/mon 3ish-10pm, closed tues.

Paradox - *1e Bloemdwarsstraat 2, 623-5639 (9)*

All the food in this unique coffeeshop is organic and the prices are quite reasonable. The staff is very friendly and the neighbourhood is beautiful. I have to admit that I haven't tried any of their smokable offerings, but I know that they make an amazing chocolate poppyseed cake! I think a lot of ex-pats hang out here, because I always hear english when I visit. Open daily 09-19:00.

Het Ballonnetje - *Roetersstraat 12, 622-8027 (10)*

This is one for those of you staying in the Sleepin area. You won't find many tourists here as it's off the beaten track: it's a good place to meet Dutch people. Het Ballonnetje is small and very cosy with wooden furniture and a tall palm tree. Upstairs in the small loft is a T.V. and a stack of games. It's a peaceful place to play cards on a rainy night. Make sure to take a look at their terrarium housing tiny fluorescent frogs! Open daily 10-22:00.

The T-Boot - *Oude Schans 143 (11)*

A coffeeshop on a houseboat: pretty cool! The inside is nothing special and I never stay in there. But in the summer, on a sunny day, it's fantastic: smoking on the big deck by the water, getting a tan, watching the ducks and boats cruise by. Located between Nieuwmarkt and Waterlooplein. In the summer open daily 10-20:00. Winter fri and sat only 10-20:00.

La Tertulia - *Prinsengracht 312 (12)*

Plants, flowers and a little fountain give this coffeeshop a tropical feeling, but what I like best about this place is the outdoor terrace in the summer. It's on a canal and there are flowers on all the tables. It's easy to find this building: just look for the Van Gogh sunflowers painted all over it. Open tues-sat 11-19:00.

Katsu - *1st Van Der Helststraat 70, 675-2617 (13)*

Katsu is an inexpensive neighbourhood coffeeshop just off the Albert Cuyp Market. It's got a shabby, homey feel to it, wicked grass, and music in the Led Zeppelin vein. Good prices too. Open mon-thurs 11-23:00, fri/sat 11-24:00, sun 12-22:00.

Coffeeshops

Dutch Flowers - *Singel 387, 624-7624 (14)*

I like this coffeeshop because it's got a great view: a beautiful canal on one side, and an interesting and busy little street on the other. There are lots of magazines and comics and good music. It's located right in the centre of the city by Spui Circle. Their impressive selection of hash is also available in small amounts. And they serve beer. Open sun-thurs 10-24:00, fri/sat 10-24:00.

The Otherside - *Reguliersdwarsstraat 6, 625-5141 (15)*

Located right in the heart of the gay ghetto. Mostly men come here, but women are also welcome. It's a friendly spot and it's easy to meet people. The main drawback is the loud dance music. There are a couple of other gay coffeeshops on this street too: The Zoo, and Downtown. Otherside open daily 10-01:00.

The Rookies - *Korte Leidsedwarsstraat 145-147, 639-0978 (16)*

One of the few coffeeshops where you can have a beer with your smoke. This mellow place is just down the street from the Leidseplein. They've got a pooltable, and an air purifier that's great for non-tobacco smokers. Open sun-thurs 13-01:00, fri/sat 13-02:00.

The Dreadlock - *Oudezijds Voorburgwal 67 (17)*

Everyone asks me to recommend a coffeeshop in the Red Light district. This is it. Kind of run down and grungy, this smoky bar suits the feeling of the neighbourhood. At the same time the staff are very friendly. And the view overlooking the canal and the old church surrounded by women in windows is quite captivating. Happy hours 20-22:00. Open mon-thurs 15-24:00, fri/sat 13-24:00, sun 14-24:00.

Fatal Flower - *Stadhouderskade 46, 679-4296 (18)*

Free coffee, bottomless cup! Now, it's not great coffee, but it's free coffee, and I think that's a pretty good gimmick. It's warm and cosy in here on a rainy day as you sit in the plant filled room and stare out over the canal view. Good location too - just a stone's throw from the Rijks-museum. Their interesting menu includes a couple of US weeds and lots of hash. Those of you who like that old Pink Floyd and Doors stuff will be happy here. Open daily 11-23:00.

Rasta Baby - *Prince Hendrikkade 6-7, 624-7403 (19)*

Reggae is best enjoyed in a blunted state and that's why I pop in here from time to time to hear a little Alpha Blondy or Prophet Bob. There's a glassed in terrace in the front and they have a bar as well. Turn right outside of Central Station and it's just two blocks away. Open sun-thurs 09:30-01:00, fri,sat 09:30-02:00.

SEEDS/GROW SHOPS

There are several places to buy seeds around town. But remember that they are sold only "for agricultural purposes within the Netherlands". In most countries it's illegal to import seeds. You've been warned.

Dutch Passion - *Nieuwezijds Voorburgwal 87A, 627-5683*

Homegrown Fantasy (see Coffeeshops, above) is home to this seed company, which stocks seed lines from Holland and the rest of the world. Wow! They started out selling mostly outdoor lines, but now carry a variety of indoor as well. Prices for these seeds, which come highly recommended by growers, are very reasonable, especially if you buy in bulk. Personally, I love their fantastic Haze/Skunk which won the 1992 Cannabis Cup Award! Open daily 12-23:00.

CIA (Cannabis In Amsterdam) - *Droogbak 2-1, 627-1646*

This wild hemp store (see Shopping section), sells seeds from all the other companies as well as their in-house line, T.H.Seeds. Stop by and consult their resident seed expert, Adam, who's always happy to give advice on seeds and growing. Open wed-sat 12-18:00, sun/mon 15-18:00, tues by appointment only.

Positronics - *Cornelius Troostraat 33, 679-7790*

In business since 1979, Positronics has everything for organic growing, from seeds to natural fertilisers to lamps they produce themselves. Beginners will find their quality seeds very affordable. This is perhaps the most fun grow shop in town because of their Sinsemilla Salon where you can listen to the Grateful Dead and "taste test" their weed! Open mon-sat 10-18:00.

Sensi Seeds - *Oudezijds Achterburgwal 150, 624-0386*

The people who brought you the Hash and Marijuana Museum run this business, too. You'll find everything you need for growing, starting with seeds. Prices are a bit high, but they have proven genetic quality. They were big winners at the 1993 and 1994 Cannabis Cup. It's worth stopping in here just to pick up their colour catalogue full of beautiful buds. Open mon-fri 11-18:00, sat 11-17:00.

Cerebral Seeds - *Available at C.I.A. (see above)*

This company burst onto the seed scene in a big way last fall, scoring high marks at the Cannabis Cup for their AK-47 and Bubblegum. They offer 6 strains in all, including Hydro Chronic, which they claim has Northern lights quality combined with Big Bud quantity. Available exclusively at C.I.A..

Home Grow Shop - *Hortusplantsoen 7, 622-0284*

There's been a Home Grow Shop in Rotterdam for quite some time and this April they opened one in Amsterdam. They are located on a quiet street just across the canal from the Botanical Gardens. They have a big selection of everything you'd need for growing as well as a variety of paraphernalia, like pipes and books. Open mon-fri 10-19:00 (thurs 'til 21:00), sat 10-17:00.

Advanced Hydroponics of Holland - *Gerard Doustraat 71, 664-9887*

If you're interested in hydroponics check out this shop. It's located near the Albert Cuyp market. Open mon 13-17:00, tues-fri 11-18:00, sat 11-17:00.

Monica in a grow room.

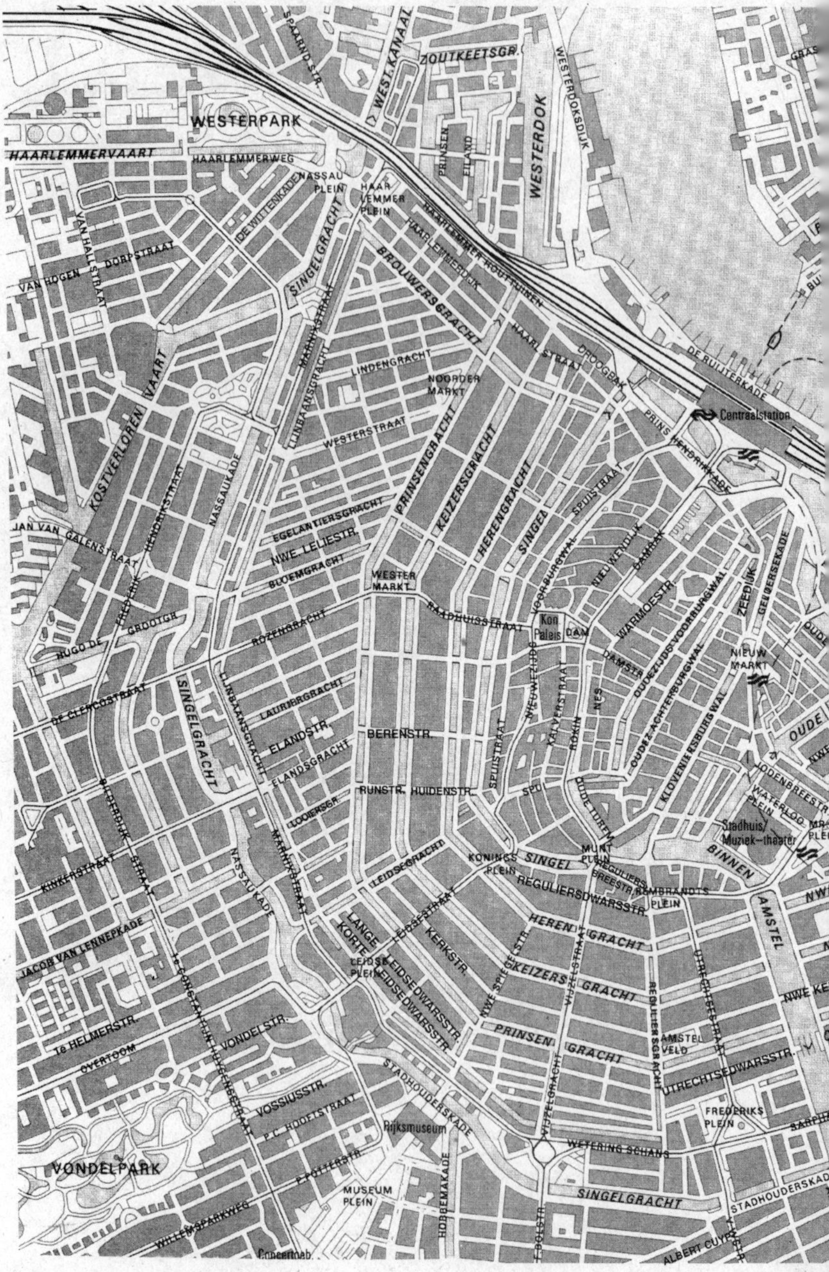
WESTERPARK
HAARLEMMERVAART
HAARLEMMERWEG
SPAARNDSTR.
WEST. KANAAL
ZOUTKEETSGR.
WESTERDOKSDIJK
WESTERDOK
PRINSEN EILAND
NASSAU PLEIN
HAAR LEMMER PLEIN
DE WITTENKADE
VAN HALLSTRAAT
DORPSTRAAT
VAN HOGEN
SINGELGRACHT
MARNIXSTRAAT
BROUWERSGRACHT
HAARLEMMER HOUTTUINEN
HAARLEMMERDIJK
HAARL. STRAAT
DROOGBAK
DE RUIJTERKADE
Centraalstation
PRINS HENDRIKKADE
LINDENGRACHT
NOORDER MARKT
WESTERSTRAAT
LIJNBAANSGRACHT
KOSTVERLOREN VAART
HENDRIKSTRAAT
NASSAUKADE
PRINSENGRACHT
KEIZERSGRACHT
HERENGRACHT
SINGEL
SPUISTRAAT
VOORBURGWAL
NIEUWENDIJK
DAMRAK
ZEEDIJK
GELDERSEKADE
JAN VAN GALENSTRAAT
EGELANTIERSGRACHT
NWE. LELIESTR.
BLOEMGRACHT
WESTER MARKT
RAADHUISSTRAAT
Kon. Paleis
DAM
WARMOESTR.
NIEUW MARKT
HUGO DE GROOTGR.
FREDERIK
ROZENGRACHT
DAMSTR.
OUDEZIJDS VOORBURGWAL
OUDEZIJDS ACHTERBURGWAL
DE CLERCQSTRAAT
LAURIERGRACHT
NIEUWEZIJDS
KALVERSTRAAT
ROKIN
NES
ELANDSTR.
BERENSTR.
ELANDSGRACHT
KLOVENIERSBURGWAL
JODENBREESTR.
WATERLOO PLEIN
RUNSTR.
HUIDENSTR.
SPUI
OUDE TURFM.
LOOIERSGR.
Stadhuis/ Muziek-theater
MUNT PLEIN
KONINGS PLEIN
SINGEL
BINNEN
KINKERSTRAAT
LEIDSEGRACHT
REGULIERS BREESTR.
REMBRANDTS PLEIN
REGULIERSDWARSSTR.
NASSAUKADE
MARNIXSTRAAT
LEIDSESTRAAT
HEREN GRACHT
AMSTEL
JACOB VAN LENNEPKADE
KERKSTR.
LANGE
KORTE
LEIDSE PLEIN
LEIDSEDWARSSTR.
NWE. SPIEGELSTR.
KEIZERS GRACHT
VIJZELSTRAAT
REGULIERSGRACHT
UTRECHTSESTRAAT
NWE KER
1e HELMERSTR.
VONDELSTR.
1e CONSTANTIJN HUYGENSSTRAAT
PRINSEN GRACHT
AMSTEL VELD
OVERTOOM
STADHOUDERSKADE
VIJZELGRACHT
UTRECHTSEDWARSSTR.
VOSSIUSSTR.
P.C. HOOFTSTRAAT
Rijksmuseum
FREDERIKS PLEIN
WETERING SCHANS
VONDELPARK
P. POTTERSTR.
HOBBEMAKADE
SINGELGRACHT
STADHOUDERSKADE
MUSEUM PLEIN
WILLEMSPARKWEG
F. BOLSTR.
ALBERT CUYPSTR.
Concertgeb.

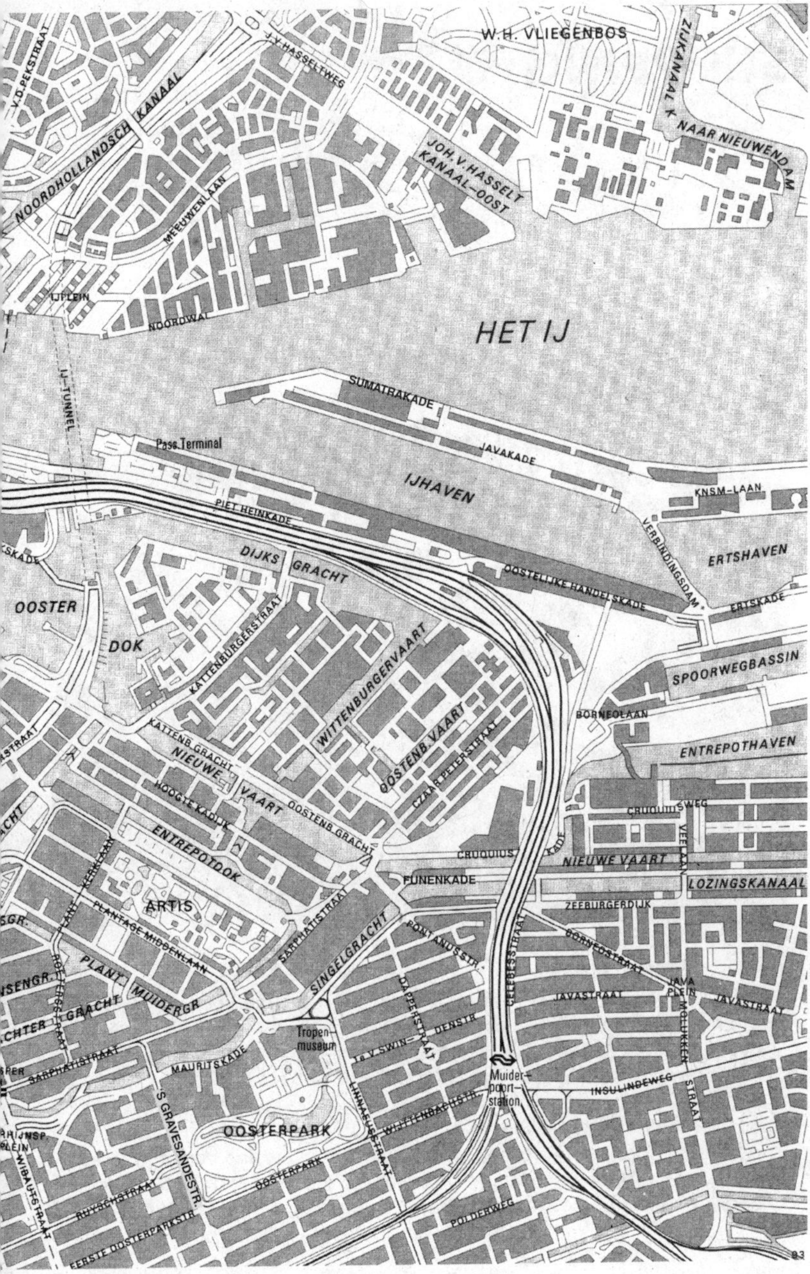
W.H. VLIEGENBOS
ZIJKANAAL K NAAR NIEUWENDAM
J.V. HASSELTWEG
V.D. PEKSTRAAT
NOORDHOLLANDSCH KANAAL
JOH. V. HASSELT KANAAL-OOST
MEEUWENLAAN
IJPLEIN
NOORDWAL
HET IJ
IJ-TUNNEL
SUMATRAKADE
Pass.Terminal
JAVAKADE
IJHAVEN
KNSM-LAAN
PIET HEINKADE
VERBINDINGSDAM
ERTSHAVEN
DIJKS GRACHT
OOSTELIJKE HANDELSKADE
ERTSKADE
OOSTER DOK
KATTENBURGERSTRAAT
WITTENBURGERVAART
SPOORWEGBASSIN
BORNEOLAAN
KATTENB. GRACHT
NIEUWE VAART
OOSTENB. VAART
CZAAR PETERSTRAAT
ENTREPOTHAVEN
HOOGTE KADIJK
OOSTENB. GRACHT
ENTREPOTDOK
CRUQUIUSWEG
VEELAAN
CRUQUIUSKADE
NIEUWE VAART
FUNENKADE
LOZINGSKANAAL
ARTIS
KERKLAAN
PLANTAGE MIDDENLAAN
SARPHATISTRAAT
SINGELGRACHT
ZEEBURGERDIJK
PONTANUSSTR.
BORNEOSTRAAT
CELEBESSTRAAT
DAPPERSTRAAT
JAVASTRAAT
JAVA PLEIN
MOLUKKENSTRAAT
PLANT. MUIDERGR.
ROETERSSTRAAT
Tropen-museum
Te V. SWINDENSTR.
MAURITSKADE
SARPHATISTRAAT
Muider-poort-station
INSULINDEWEG
LINNAEUSSTRAAT
WITTENBACHSTR.
'S GRAVESANDESTR.
OOSTERPARK
RUYSCHSTRAAT
WIBAUTSTRAAT
EERSTE OOSTERPARKSTR.
POLDERWEG

SHOPPING

Saturday at 17:00 or 18:00 stores in Amsterdam lock their doors and most don't open again until mid-day monday. On sundays and at night the only place to buy food other than restaurants is at night shops (see Food section). This year, under a new law, about 40 shops in designated "tourist areas" will be open on sunday.

MARKETS

Bazaar Attitude - *Mystèr 2000, Lijnbaansgracht 92, 620-3578*

From their press release: "Bazaar Attitude is a club market - a funky mix of live performances, d.j.s, a cybercafé and 3-D cinema. As well as a market of over 50 stalls. [We] offer unique and original fashion and accessories, gifts and artwork. You may want to get your tarot cards read, have your hair cut, enjoy a back massage, chinese face massage, or reflexology. Work out on our brain machine. Maybe you'd like to hook up to the internet in our cybercafé, or just take a break, drink our fresh juices and be entertained by our live performances throughout the day - from jazz and poetry to african dance and drag." Mystèr 2000 (see Live Venues, Music section) is a new location for Bazaar Attitude which was a weekly event last year, and always a lot of fun. Happens the last sunday of every month. Entrance ƒ5.

Albert Cuypmarkt - *Albert Cuypstraat*

It's big and it's great! Amsterdam's most famous market is crowded with stalls and shoppers. You'll find everything here from fruits and veggies, to clothes and hardware. Underwear is a good deal and so are plain cotton t-shirts (if yours are getting smelly). Just remember that you don't pick your own fruit and the vendors will often try to slip in a couple of rotten ones. This happens to tourists and Dutch shoppers alike, so don't be afraid to complain. Open mon-sat 09-16:30.

Boerenmarkt - *Noordermarkt*

Its location in the courtyard of the old Noorderkerk lends a medieval feel to this organic market. All the booths sell healthy produce and products. Consequently, it's not really cheap, but if you like markets it's well worth a visit. Right around the corner is the Lindengracht market (see below). Another organic market that also takes place on saturdays is at the Nieuwemarkt from 09-16:00. The Noordermarkt is open sat 09-15:00.

Lindenmarkt - *Lindengracht*

This is an all purpose market that's a bit more expensive than Albert Cuyp, but still has good deals. It's in a beautiful neighbourhood and is right around the corner from the organic Boerenmarkt. Open sat 09-15:00.

Noordermarkt - *Noordermarkt*

For all you die-hard shoppers with nowhere else to go on monday morning, this market's for you. Clothes, books, records, and all kinds of junk. Great for relaxed browsing. Open mondays 09-12:00.

Dappermarkt - *Dapperstraat*

A lot of immigrants from North Africa and the Middle East shop at this all purpose market, which is the cheapest in Amsterdam. There's even a resident Elvis impersonator (Vegas years). If you're staying at the Sleepin it's the closest big market. Open mon-sat 09-16:00.

Waterlooplein Market - *Waterlooplein*

This square is home to a terrific flea market where you can find clothes and jewellery and all kinds of junk. Depending on where you're from, this can be a good place to find used leather jackets. It's easy to spend a couple of hours wandering around and, unlike other Amsterdam markets, you can (and should) bargain. Open mon-sat 10-17:00.

De Rommelmarkt - *Looiersgracht 38*

From the entrance, this flea market appears to be just a small storefront, but if you go in you'll find a sprawling 2 floors of junk. It's a lot of fun even if it's not the cheapest of markets. Mondays - stamps, coins and cards. Tuesdays - books, records, etc. Wednesdays - everything. Thursdays - second hand clothes. Fridays - closed. Saturdays - everything. Sundays - antiques. Open 11-17:00.

Flower Market - *Singel Canal*

This pretty market is full of flowers and plants sold from barges on the Singel canal between Koningsplein and Muntplein. There are lots of good deals and it's probably the best place to buy tulip bulbs. Even if you're not interested in shopping here, it's nice to wander through. Mon-sat 09-17:00.

Street Vendors

In the summer many street vendors sell artwork and Indian/ Thai/ African clothes and jewellery in the tunnel under the Rijksmuseum and also in the Vondelpark (see Hanging Out section). Sometimes you can find interesting stuff. If you want to sell something in one of these places you'll find that the cops are usually pretty relaxed. If they want you to move they generally give you 5 or 10 minutes to pack up. It's smart to do what they say and be gone before they come back: your goods can be confiscated.

BOOKS & MAGAZINES

Kok Antiquariaat - *Oude Hoogstraat 14-18, 623-1191*

One of the best used bookstores in Amsterdam. Spacious and well organised. Lots and lots of English. Make sure you look upstairs as well, and in the basement where all the bargain books and magazines are piled high. Open mon-fri 09:30-18:00, sat 09:30-17:00.

Van Gennep - *Nieuwezijds Voorburgwal 330, 626-4448*

A fantastic "remainder" bookstore with the best prices for new books in Amsterdam. They have an impressive collection of quality english books, and prices start as low as ƒ4. Great for bargain hunting. Near Spui circle. Open mon-fri 10-18:00 (thurs 'til 21:00), sat 10-17:00.

Vrolijk - *Paleisstraat 135, 623-5142*

This shop advertises itself as "the largest gay and lesbian bookstore on the continent". It's located just off the Dam Square and it's usually pretty busy. If you're looking for something special, the staff are friendly and helpful. Open mon 11-18:00, tue-fri 10-18:00 (thurs 'til 21:00), sat 10-17:00.

Books & magazines

Vrouwen in Druk - *Westermarkt 5, 623-5854*
A small womens' bookstore across from the beautiful old Westerkerk and the Homo Monument. Mostly used books as well as magazines and postcards. Open tues-sat 11-18:00.

Antiquariaat Lorelei - *Prinsengracht 495, 623-4308*
Used books by and about women. Located in a cosy, canal-front shop. Open tues-sat 12-17:00.

Intermale - *Spuistraat 251, 625 0009*
This is a gay bookstore. It's a nice space with a good selection of books, magazines and some videos. They have gay guides to countries all around the world and a small porno section in the back. Open mon 12-18:00; tues-sat 10-18:00; thurs 10-21:00.

American Discount Book Center - *Kalverstraat 185, 625-5537*
I think this is the cheapest store for new books, especially for students who get a 10% discount. Huge selection. Look for bargain books in the basement. The Kalverstraat is one of the biggest shopping streets in the city (no cars allowed).

Lambiek - *Kerkstraat 78, 626-7543*

This is the best comic bookstore in Amsterdam. New, used and fanzine comics too. It's interesting to look over all the European comix and they've got lots of Canadian and American stuff as well. Open mon-fri 11-18:00; sat 11-17:00.

Evenaar - *Singel 348, 624-6289*

It's not cheap, but this travel bookshop has a fascinating collection. Works are organised by region and include not only guides and journals, but novels, political analyses and history - many by lesser known authors. Worth visiting for a browse if you're travelling onward from Amsterdam. Open mon-fri 12-18:00, sat 11-17:00.

J. de Slegte Boekhandel - *Kalverstraat 48-52, 622-5933*

Some good deals on remainders can be found at this big store on the Kalverstraat. It lacks the charm of KOK (see above), but upstairs you'll find a huge selection of used books, many in english. Open mon 11-18:00, tues-fri 09:30-18:00, sat 09:30-18:00.

Athenaeum Nieuwscentrum - *Spui 14-16, 623-3933*

For cheap magazines check the bargain bin at this news shop on Spui Circle. I've found lots of good stuff here in the ƒ1-ƒ2 range. For new magazines this is one of the best stores in Amsterdam. The sister bookstore next door is excellent, but not cheap. Open mon-sat 08-22:00, sun 10-18:00.

Leeshal Oost - *Commelinstraat*

Piles and piles of old magazines overflow the shelves of this shop near the Tropenmuseum (see Museum section). It's a good place for collectors. I found a first edition *Punk Magazine* with a good Lou Reed interview for only ƒ3. I'm gonna keep it, but I could sell it for a lot more.

Het Fort Van Sjakoo - *Jodenbreestraat 24, 625-8979*

"Specialises in Libertarian and radical ideas from the first to the fifth world and beyond". In addition to political books from around the world, this shop has a whole wall of fanzines and magazines, including lots of info on squatting. Also: cards, shirts and, in the basement, the independent Staalplaat (see Record Stores in this section). Open mon-sat 12-18:00.

Cultural - *Gasthuismolensteeg 4*

Here you'll find a big pile of old *Life* magazines from the 50s, and 60s starting at ƒ2.50 each. The nice old guy who owns the place also has a few shelves of english paperbacks.

Cine-Qua-Non - *Staalstraat 14, 625-5588*
New and used books and magazines all about film. Lots of good stuff to browse through here, including posters and cards. Another place to look for this kind of stuff is The Silver Screen (Haarlemmerdijk 94). Open tues-sat 13-18:00.

Oudemanhuis Boekenmarkt - *Oudemanhuispoort*
A little book market running through a covered alleyway between the Oudezijds Achterburgwal and the Kloveniersburgwal. Used books and magazines in several languages are laid out on tables and stands. Also magazines, cards and, recently, some funny etchings of pornography from centuries past for ƒ1-ƒ2. Open mon-sat 10-16:00.

The Book Exchange - *Kloveniersburgwal 58, 626-6266*
The day I went in here there was a weirdo misogynist behind the counter. But he pays the most for used books, so if you've got any to sell bring them here to the weirdo. Open mon-fri 10-18:00, sat 10-17:00.

RECORDS, TAPES & CDs

Get Records - *Utrechtsestraat 105, 622-3441*
I love this street and this is one of my favourite record stores. They have a very select, up-to-date collection of punk, rap, metal, etc.. Mostly CDs now, but still some vinyl. Open mon 12-18:00, tues-fri 10-18:00 (thurs 'til 21:00), sat 10-17:00.

Staalplaat - *Jodenbreestraat 24, 625-4176*
You'll find this store appropriately located in a stark concrete basement (only a block from the Waterlooplein flea market). It has a huge selection of underground music: industrial, experimental, electronic, noise. They do mail order world-wide. Upstairs is a great political bookstore (see Bookstores, this section). This is also a good place to look for posters advertising punk shows (though you won't find punk music here), and underground parties. Unfortunately the staff can be pretty snotty. The nicest person works on mondays. Open mon-fri 11-18:00, sat 11-17:00.

Forever Changes - *Bilderdijkstraat 148, 612-6378*
This is a well-stocked store full of new and used records and CDs. They have really interesting stuff in several sections: 60s, punk, blues, etc.. And check out the singles boxes on the counter. There are also some fanzines. Open mon 13-18:00, Tues-fri 10-18:00, sat 10-17:00.

Boudisque - *Haringpakkerssteeg 10-18, 623-2603*

One of Amsterdam's best record stores. They have a big selection and they know what's hot. Lots of punk and grunge and metal as well as music from all around the world on vinyl and CD. Open mon 13-18:00, tues-fri 10-18:0, sat 10-17:00.

Concerto - *Utrechtsestraat 54-60, 624-5467*

New and used records, tapes and CDs in a great neighbourhood. Good prices on used stuff. Big selection. Well worth checking out. Open mon-fri 11-18:00, tue-fri 10-18:00 (thurs 'til 21:00), sat 10-17:00.

Back Beat Records - *Egelantiersstraat 19, 627-1657*

Jazz, soul, funk, pop, blues, R+B: there's a lot packed into this store's three levels. It's located in the Jordaan. Open mon-fri 11-18:00, sat 10-18:00.

Record Palace - *Weteringschans 33, 622-3904*

This is another good place for collectors; they have sections for most kinds of music. It's located not far from the famous Paradiso (see Music section). Open mon-fri 11-18:00, sat 11-17:00.

The Sound of the Fifties - *Prinsengracht 669, 623-9745*

This nice, old store has a great collection of just what it's name says. Also a source of info on fan clubs and appreciation societies. Open mon-fri 10-18:00, sat 10-17:00.

Distortion Records - *Westerstraat 72, 627-0004*

Amsterdam's newest record shop. They advertise "loads of noise, lo-fi, punkrock, and indie". Collectors, especially of vinyl, are going to love this place. The owners here are definitely on top of things. They're located just up the street from the Noorderkerk. Open tues-sat 10-18:00 (thurs 'til 21:00).

CLUB FASHIONS

Amsterdam's club fashion shops stock a wide variety of designers both international and, more interesting I think, local. These are all good places to find information on parties and raves.

ZX - *Kerkstraat 113, 620-8567*

ZX is located in a cool storefront on the Kerkstraat. It's a welcoming place where the staff are genuinely friendly and helpful. A lot of interesting clothing designs are available here as well as magazines, knicks, knacks and, of course, party info. In the back you'll find the Hair Police (see below). Open mon-fri 12-18:00 (thurs 'til 19:00), sat 11-17:00.

Trancedome - *Nieuwe Zijds Voorburgwal 351, 625-2157*
This is a friendly, busy shop with a great location in the centre. There are lots of photos of past raves, wild hats, accessories, tapes, and more. Want something made to order? Bring in your designs. Open mon-sat 11-18:00 (thurs 'til 20:00).

Diablo - *Oudezijds Voorburgwal 242, 623-4506*
Lots of interesting clothing and accessories await you in this dark, grungy store. Even if you're not into the full-volume metal blasting from the speakers, you'll find something new and different. I like all the skeleton jewellery and the hand-cuff earrings. Open mon-fri 10:30-18:00 (thurs 'til 21:00), sat 10-17:00.

MISCELLANEOUS

The Head Shop - *Kloveniersburgwal 39, 624-9061*
Most, if not all, your drug paraphernalia needs can be met in shops on the streets heading east off Dam square past the Grand Hotel Krasnapolsky (which, by the way, has very nice, clean toilets upstairs to the left off the lobby). I think the best store is The Head Shop, which has been in business since 1968. Lots and lots of pipes, bongs and papers; plus books, magazines, postcards, stickers and the required collection of incense and Indian clothing. It has a good reputation and sometimes gets very crowded. Open mon 13-18:00, tues-fri 11-18:00, sat 11-17:00.

Green Lands Hemp Store - *Utrechtsestraat 26, 625-1100*
Jeans, jackets, shirts, hats and other clothing... made from hemp. Shampoo, soap, lotions... made from hemp. Writing paper, envelopes, edibles, everything in this store... made from hemp. That's hemp as in the plant that produces cannabis. These things make great gifts. Do yourself and this old planet a favour by visiting this store and finding out more about this amazing plant and it's myriad of uses. Open mon 13-18:00, tues-fri 11-18:00, sat 11-17:00.

3-D Holograms - *Grimburgwal 2, 624-7225*
This shop is almost a gallery and, in fact, the owners are planning to open a hologram museum. There are some great works of art here and a good selection of inexpensive hologram jewellery, stickers, cards, etc.. You might

want to take a look if you have to buy some presents for all those loved ones back home. There's also a good pancake place upstairs (see Restaurants, Food section). Open tues-sat 12-18:00.

Humana - *Gravenstraat 22, 623-3214*

If you like shopping for used clothes, stop by this store. It's really hit and miss. Sometimes they have only shit, but I've also found some fantastic deals on all kinds of stuff: perfect Levis for ƒ18, a leather jacket for ƒ35, and once they had a big rummage sale and I bought a tv for ƒ12! The money goes to third world development projects. Open mon 13-18:00, tues-fri 09:30-18:00, sat 09:30-17:00.

Louise's Tattoo Parlor - *Stromarkt 13, 688-0258*

Louise has 12 years experience as a tattoo artist, including a stint with Hanky Panky (see below). Check out her work and you'll see she's adept at all styles: traditional, tribal, free hand, bright colours, etc. Her basement shop opened this spring in the same building as Absolute Danny (see Sex Shops, Sex section), and right next door to Body Manipulations (see below). The Stromarkt is getting cooler by the minute. Open mon 13-18:00, tues-sat 12-18:00.

Hanky Panky Tattooing - *Oudezijds Voorburgwal 141, 627-4848*

Hanky Panky is located in the back of the Tattoo Museum (see Museum section). The international staff are very knowledgeable about their art. The selection is immense and of course you're welcome to bring in your own design. Lots of famous rock-stars (too many to name-drop), come here and that's only going to make this place more popular than it already is. There's also a selection of books and postcards available. Go early to make an appointment. Be patient. Open mon-sat 11-18:00.

Body Manipulations - *Stromarkt 11, 623-3442 (piercing studio)*
Oude Hoog Straat 31, 420-8085 (piercing, permanent cosmetics)

"A piercing studio, scarification, branding". This is the sister store to the one in San Francisco. Along with tattoos, piercing is probably the most popular form of body art. If you want something done you should head for this place. The people who run the studio are more than happy to talk to you about the procedure and what pain (if any), is involved. They also have an excellent collection of books and magazines on the subject. Prices start at ƒ15 for an ear piercing (incl. stud), cartilage ƒ30. Lip or eyebrow ƒ40. Tongue, nipple, navel, clit, penis, etc, ƒ50 (excl. jewellery). Open tues-sat 12-18:00.

Conscious Dreams - *Kerkstraat 117, 626-6907*

It's always worth *dropping* into this gallery/shop to see the changing art and design exhibitions. In the back you'll find a large selection of smart drinks and drugs. They have all kinds, some that you might not know about, and they're more than happy to advise and inform you on their different uses. It's a very trippy place. Come in... and be experienced. Open tues-fri 11-18:30, sat 11-17:30.

Vibes - *Singel 10, 622-3962*
This store's dope, with all the cool skate, hip hop, and graffiti labels out of the States; plus skate equipment, and t-shirts by locals TBH. AND it's the only place in town that carries the Beastie Boys' magazine, *Grand Royal*. Open mon 13-18:00, tues-fri 11-18:00 (thurs 'til 21:00), sat 10-15:00.

C.I.A. (Cannabis In Amsterdam) - *Droogbak 2-1, 627-1646*
Turn right outside of Central Station, cross over the bridge at the Singel canal, walk up the stairs at this address, and you've arrived at C.I.A. Headquarters. This is one of the most happening shops in Amsterdam and old J. Edgar is rolling over in his grave. Working out of this cool, old warehouse, C.I.A. "agents" sell books, hemp products, seeds (see Cannabis section), and more. Anyone who wants to find out about cannabis, here in the Netherlands or anywhere else in the world, will find lots of "declassified" educational documents on display. Open wed-sat 12-18:00, sun/mon 15-18:00, tues by appointment only.

Kelere Kelder - *Prinsengracht 285*
Kelere is Amsterdam slang for clothes and kelder means cellar. Not surprisingly then, you'll find this cool used clothes store in the cellar of a longstanding squat on the Prinsengracht. Except for some new political t-shirts with unique designs, everything else in the store is used. There are racks of clothes, some books, records, other odds and ends, and even a basket of give-aways! Prices are very cheap, so you probably won't come away empty handed. They may open more often in tourist season, but for the moment it's only open sat/sun 12-18:00.

Front Line - *Prins Hendrikkade 10, 623-0143*
Feeling irie? Drop by this reggae shop across the street from Central Station. They sell CD's, clothing, postcards, buttons, and a selection of pipes. They also have info on who's jamming around town. Stay positive. Open mon 13-18:00, tues-fri 09:30-18:00 (thurs 'til 21:00), sat 09:30-17:00.

De Vlo - *Bloemgracht 197, 624-0021*
If you like collecting things like old records and movie star photos then this is the place for you. All kinds of books and knick-knacks crowd this pretty little store in the Jordaan. Don't bother asking about the Brigitte Bardot album though, it's not for sale. Open only wed and thurs 11-17:00, fri and sat 10-17:00.

De Derde Winkel - *Huidenstraat 16, 625-2245*

Books, clothes, crafts, etc. from developing countries. It's not the cheapest store, but there are some deals and the money is going back to the right people. Open mon 13-18:00, tues-fri 10-18:00 (thurs 'til 21:00), sat 10-17:00.

Hair Police
Kerkstraat 113, 620-8567

What are you thinking about? Extensions? Dreadlocks? Weaves or braids? Or maybe just a haircut? You should do it while you're in Amsterdam. George Clinton had his funky hair worked on at the Minneapolis Hair Police. What better recommendation could you have? They're located in ZX (see Club Fashions, this section) and prices are very reason-able. Open mon-fri 12-18:00 (thurs 'til 21:00), sat 11-17:00.

Under the knife at the Hair Police.

Herenkapsalon - *Ferdinand Bolstraat 4, 671-2640*

If you just want a little off the top, this is about the cheapest haircut in town (only f16.50). It's a mens' place, but they'll cut women's hair too. Right across the street from the Heineken Brewery (see Museum section). Open mon 08:30-16:00, tues closed, wed-fri 08:30-17:00, sat 08:30-16:00.

Stilett - *Damstraat 14, 625-2854*

This is a big t-shirt store that plays loud punk, some metal, and hip hop. They've got lots of unique designs that you won't find elsewhere: political, psychedelic, phunky, funny. Open mon-sat 11-18:00.

The Old Man - *Damstraat 16, 627-0043*

This is another drug paraphernalia shop with a wide choice of pipes. Walk to the back and you'll come upon a baffling array of weapons. Some of you might be more comfortable upstairs where they sell snowboards and frisbees: things more compatible with smoking. Open mon-sat 09-18:00 (thurs 'til 21:00).

Miscellaneous

China Town Slijterij - *Geldersekade 94-96, 624-5229*

For some reason I think that this liquor store is cheaper than others, but I don't know if it's true. Anyway, it's where I buy my booze and a couple of doors down is a great Chinese supermarket. Open mon-sat 09-18:00.

De Witte Tandenwinkel - *Runstraat 5, 623-3443*

I love the window of this store. They have the worlds largest collection of toothbrushes! All shapes, all sizes and styles. Take a look if you're in the neighbourhood. Open mon 13-16:00, tues-fri 10-18:00, sat 10-17:00.

De Roos - *Vondelstraat 35-37, 689-0081*

If you're into alternative health care this centre might interest you. It's located in an old house just north of Vondelpark and is home to an alternative health care shop, practitioners' rooms, and a café. Check the bulletin board in the basement for info about events in the community or talk to the staff at the reception desk. De Roos sometimes host a smoke-free disco on saturday nights 22:30-02:00. Open mon-fri 08-23:00, sat 09-18:00 and 20-01:00, sun 09-18:00.

Salvation Army Shop - *Rozengracht 198*

Used clothes, books, furniture, and all sorts of other crap. It's a real thrift store: prices are cheap and it smells like a locker room. Don't make a special trip here, but if you're in the neighbourhood and you like bargain hunting then stop in. Open mon/wed/thurs 09:30-12:00 and 13-16:00, fri 09:30-14:00, closed sat/sun/tues.

Studio Spui - *Spui 4, 623-6926*

Check this shop for good specials on film close to its expiry date. Open mon 10-17:30, tues-fri 09-17:30 (thurs 'til 21:00), sat 10-17:30.

Dirk van den Broek - *Look in the phonebook*

Dirk van den Broek is a supermarket chain that also does photo processing. It takes two days and I had a roll of 24 colour prints done for $f11$. This is a good price, but there aren't any Dirk van den Broeks right in the centre of town. More expensive and easier to find is Hema Photo (Kalverstraat 200). Passport size photo booths can be found at the main post office (Singel 250), and at Central Station for $f6$-$f7$.

HANGING OUT

This is the section for people who enjoy just wandering about the streets, seeing who's around, listening to music in the park, and for these of you who are really broke. During the warm months the streets and parks of Amsterdam come alive and you don't need a lot of money to find entertainment. I've also got a couple of suggestions for when it's rainy or cold.

VONDELPARK

When the weather is warm this is the most happening place in the city. Crowds of people wander throughout the park enjoying the sunshine and the circus-like atmosphere. Walk along the main pathways lined with people selling cakes and clothes, jewellery and joints. Notice the tarot and palm readers sitting peacefully in the shade of the trees. And all the jugglers practising with plates and balls and bowling pins, who look like jesters from a medieval court (especially if you've just had a smoke). Wander further into the park past old men fishing in quiet ponds and into the rose garden for an olfactory overload. Come out on the other side and by a large field of cows and goats and even a llama! It's easy to forget you're in a city. About now you may want to look for one of the cafés in the park in order to buy an ice cream. While you lick, listen to some music or watch a play in the band-shell, or to one of the dozens of musicians and bands jamming throughout the park. Look at the bright coloured parrots (I'm not kidding), in the trees. Or maybe you just want to join all the other people laying half-dressed on the grass, reading, smoking, playing chess, or just sleeping.

LEIDSEPLEIN

I mention this square in the music section as a place to catch street musicians. If the weather is good it's also great for street performers who sometimes line up for their chance to entertain the throngs of tourists (and make some dough). A lot of these artists are very talented and you can see their professionalism as they work the crowds between each unicycling, fire-eating, juggling trick, and how they deal with the inevitable disruptive drunk. If you do have a good time watching these people be sure to drop a guilder in the hat.

DAM SQUARE

Quiet in the winter, but almost always something going on in the summer. Keep your eyes open. And don't buy any drugs from the scummy dealers here: you'll definitely get ripped off. Look instead for a coffeeshop listed in the Cannabis section of this book.

LIBRARY
main branch Prinsengracht 587, 523-0900

You have to be a member to take books out, but there's a lot to do here anyway. If you ask at the information desk inside they'll give you english newspapers and magazines like *Time* and *Newsweek* to read. It's a good way to catch up on news if you've been travelling for awhile. They also have interesting photo exhibitions on the ground floor. In the cafetaria you'll find more newspapers and magazines from around the world, many in English. On the second floor there's a good selection of English novels and any other section in the library will also have a lot of English books and magazines. Comix are on the second floor. The travel section on the third floor has a whole shelf of books about Holland and any other country you might be heading to. One floor up from there is a music section with lots of magazines. Finally, if you're looking for a flat or need to sell something, the bulletin board in the front entrance is well used. Open mon-13-21:00, tues-thurs 10-21:00, fri/sat 10-17:00, open sun oct-mar 13-17:00.

SNOOKER

Docksider - *Entrepotdok 7-10, 626-9349*

There's nowhere I know to play free snooker, but on weekdays between 11-18:00 you can play here for 1/2 price. That comes to ƒ7.50 an hour per table no matter how many people are playing: trust me, it's a sweet deal. The atmosphere is snooker and the tables are prima. Call to make sure this special is still on.

De Keizers Snooker Club - *Herengracht 256, 623-1586*

Everyday from 13-19:00 you can play snooker or pool here for ƒ8.50 an hour.

VIRGIN MEGASTORE
Nieuwe Zijds Voorburgwal 182, 622-8929

The Magna Plaza opened three years ago and is worth stepping into just to see the beautiful old building that used to house the main post office. Amidst all the upscale boutiques is the Virgin Megastore, which used to be one of the best hanging out places in the city centre. It's gone down-hill since they moved into the basement, but I still come in from time to time and check the place out. There are still a few free video games. Just don't come when schools let out or you'll have to fight the little kids for a turn. On the other side of the store in the video section are 4 or 5 small screens with headphones showing all kinds of movies. There used to be more and the videos changed more often. Maybe they got tired of me standing there watching for two hours. Lots of new CD releases are played on little stands with headphones. Or pick any CD and bring it to the counter. They'll let you hear anything and you get to read the little booklet. Listen to the CD and then tell them it's not what you wanted after all. They don't care: they get paid whether you buy or not. Before you leave stop by the book section and read a few of those magazines that are too expensive to buy (unfortunately, they got rid of the bargain bin). Open mon 11-18:00, tues-fri 09:30- 18:00, sat 09:30-17:00.

GARDENS

The public gardens behind the Rijksmuseum are a pleasant, uncrowded place to sit and relax with a joint. The Stedelijk (modern art) Museum has a sculpture garden out back near Museumplein to which admission is free. Finally, you wouldn't really hang out in the Begijnhof, but it's a beautiful, old part of Amsterdam that should be seen. Look for an entrance behind the Amsterdam Historical Museum. There is also an entrance off Spui. You'll find an arched doorway between Nieuwezijds Voorburgwal and the Esprit Café. Inside that entrance you'll find an interesting plaque describing the history of this pretty courtyard.

HOOPS

If you want to play a little basketball, join a game on the courts at Museumplein or head to the Malle Monkey squat (see Restaurants, Food section). There is also a court on the Marnixstraat across from Gary's Muffins (see Cafés section), which isn't great, but is worth noting because it's got Holland's first hemp basketball net!

SKATEBOARDING

Museumplein has two ramps that are always open to the public. The really good skaters and rollerbladers are doing some mind-blowing things these days. Down by the RAI convention centre (look on your map, it's a big building in south Amsterdam), you'll find skaters doing some good shit. Stop in at Vibes (see Shopping section), and they'll tell you what's up. Graffiti-heads should take tram line 14 to the last stop at Flevopark. Walk through the underpass away from the school and turn right. The big bridge supports under the highway make up a gallery of artists' work.

KITE FLYING

Because it's flat and windy, Holland is a great country for kite flying. A growing number of people are actually travelling with kites. All kinds can be bought at the following stores and prices start very low.

Vliegertuig - *Gasthuismolensteeg 8, 623-3450*

Open mon 11-18:00, tues 12-18:00, wed 11-18:00, thurs 12-21:00, fri 12-18:00, sat 11-18:00.

Joe's Vliegerwinkel - *Nieuwe Hoogstraat 19, 625-0139*

Open mon 13-18:00, tues-fri 11-18:00, sat 11-17:00.

High and Free - *1e Bloemdwarsstraat 13, 622-1243*

Open tues-sun 11-17:30.

Wind Mee - *Haarlemmerstraat 99, 638-9767*

Open mon 13-18:00, tues-fri 10-18:00 (thurs 'til 20:30), sat 10-17:00.

SAUNA

Sauna Fenomeen - *1e Schinkelstraat 14, 671-6780*

In spite of the fact that this is a squat sauna, this health club is clean, modern, and well equipped. It's located in a courtyard complex known as the Binnenpret (which means an "in" joke), and people of all ages, shapes and sizes come here. When you enter give your name and get a locker key from the reception on the right. On the left is a changeroom with instructions and rules in both English and Dutch. You can bring your own towel or rent one there for $f1.50$. Then get naked, have a shower, and try out the big sauna or the turkish steam bath! There is also a café serving fresh fruit, sandwiches, juices and teas. It's a relaxing place to unwind and read the paper or just listen to music and veg. Also available at extra charges are massages, tranquillity tanks, and tanning beds. Monday is for women only, and the rest of the week is mixed. Thurs/sat/sun are smoke-free. The price if you're finished before 19:00 is $f9$. After that it's $f12$. You can also buy a five or ten visit card that makes it even cheaper. Located just past the western end of Vondelpark. Open daily 14-23:00.

MUSEUMS

There are so many museums in this city that it could take you weeks to see them all. As you probably don't have that much time I'm only going to tell you about the more interesting, lesser-known museums: ones that aren't listed in every tourist brochure. For basic information about some of the big ones like the Rijksmuseum and the Van Gogh museum check the end of this section.

The Sex Museum - *Damrak 18, 622-8376*

It's true that you could see almost everything here in the Red Light district for free; on the other hand admission is only ƒ3.95 and it's fun to tell your friends you went to the Sex Museum. Some of the exhibits are really run down, but the pornography from the turn of the century is nicely displayed. The best part of the museum is the 7 foot high penis chair where you can sit and have your picture taken. Don't forget your camera! Open daily 10-23:00.

The Erotic Museum - *Oude Zijds Achterburgwal 54, 624-7303*

Much more interesting than the Sex Museum. Entrance is ƒ5. The collection is large (covers 5 floors) and varied, but unfortunately most of it is unlabelled. They have drawings by John Lennon, collages from Madonna's *Sex*, and a very ugly pornotoon from Germany that's hilarious. You can also push a button that sets a dozen or so vibrators into action! There is a floor of hardcore videos and phone sex, and above that a rather tame S+M room. Inexcusably absent are any references to gay male sex, a surprising omission considering Amsterdam's status as the gay capital of Europe. Maybe mention it on your way out. Open daily 11-01:00.

The Hash Marihuana Hemp Museum - *Oude Zijds Achterburgwal 148, 623-5961*

The addition of the word hemp to this museum's name came after a major renovation and updating of the collection by Chris Conrad, author of the book *Hemp: Lifeline to the Future*. At the entrance you'll find pamphlets and booklets on hemp and its uses, many of which are free. They also have books, magazines and hemp products for sale, including seeds which are supplied by their next door neighbour Sensi Seeds (see Cannabis section).

The exhibit consists of photos, documents, videos and artefacts dealing with all aspects of the amazing hemp plant including: history, medicinal uses, cannabis culture and even a grow room. They also have a reference library you can use. The verdict? Well worth the six guilder entrance fee (even though they fired me), but they should have a student discount. Open mon-sat 11-22:00, sun 11-17:00.

Heineken Brewery - *Stadhouderskade 78, 568-8233*
This place was better when it was a working brewery and it only cost ƒ.50 to get in. Now the price is ƒ2 (which goes to UNICEF) for a tour of Heineken history and the beer making process. Be sure to ask your guide about the kidnapping of Freddie Heineken! At the end of the tour you get what you really came for: a half hour of all the beer you can drink and a plate of cheezies. If it's your birthday you get a free mug. Tours begin at 09:30 and 11:00 mon-fri and tickets should be purchased early. Closed weekends.

Tropenmuseum - *Linnaeusstraat 2, 568-8200*
This is one of the big ones that's in every other guide book, but I'm including it here because it's such an amazing place, yet many visitors choose to skip it. This beautiful old building lies in eastern Amsterdam and houses a fantastic collection of artefacts and exhibits about the developing world. The permanent exhibition uses model villages, music, slide shows, and lots of push-button, hands-on displays giving you a feel for everyday life in these countries. There are also changing exhibitions in the central hall and photo gallery. At the entrance you'll find listings for films and music in the adjoining Souterijn theatre (see Film section), but they're not included in the admission price. Adults ƒ7.50, students ƒ4. Open mon-fri 10-17:00, sat/sun 12-17:00.

The Torture Museum - *Leidsestraat 27, 620-4070*
Don't leave Amsterdam without visiting this unique collection of torture instruments. It's very educational. You'll learn where expressions like "putting on the pressure" originated. The Museum is laid out nicely in an old house painted like a dungeon. Each object is accompanied by a small plaque explaining it's function, and by and on whom it was inflicted. Detailed drawings illustrate their use. If you aren't already aware of christianity's bloody history this is the place to see, quite graphically, just what has been done to people in the name of "god". (And speaking of god, what do you get when you cross an agnostic, an insomniac, and a dyslexic? Someone who stays up all night wondering if there's a dog.) Adults ƒ7,50, students ƒ5.50. Open daily 10-22:00 Jul-Oct, daily 10-19:00 Nov-Jun.
NOTE: *Shit! At the time of publication the Torture Museum had just closed, allegedly for non-payment of rent. Hopefully they'll open again soon.*

De Poezenboot (Cat Boat) - *a houseboat on the Singel opposite #40*

Attention cat lovers! This isn't really a museum, but what the fuck. Spend some time on this boat playing with dozens of love hungry stray cats who now have a home thanks to donations from the public and volunteers who help out here. The boat is free to visit, but you are expected to make a contribution on your way out. Grab a postcard for your cat back home. Open daily 13-15:00.

Tattoo Museum - *Oude Zijds Voorburgwal 141, 627-4848*

Welcome to a very cool museum. Step down the stairs into a gallery of tattoo needles and designs from around the world. The walls are lined with photos of tattooed and scarified bodies. Work your way slowly to the back where the good music is coming from and you'll find Hanky Panky Tattooing, (see Shopping section). Free. Open mon-sat 11-18:00.

The Museum of Florescent Art - *2nd Leliedwarsstraat 5*

At the moment this place is just a little gallery/shop called Electric Ladyland. They exhibit florescent paintings, mobiles, and sculptures (all created on the premises!), but also sell things like fractal buttons and cards. When present work on the museum is finished it's going to be very interesting. Take a look if you're wandering in the Jordaan, but don't go out of your way because it's only open sometimes.

Coffee and Tea Museum - *Warmoesstraat 67, 624-0683*

I didn't find the collection of coffee-grinders and roasters terribly exciting, but it sure smelled great in the second floor of this coffee store. Then two nice old guys gave me a cup of joe and told me some stories about the good old colonial days. Open tues/fri/sat 14-16:30.

Vrolijk Museum - *Meibergdreef 15, 566-9111 (beeper 841)*

I haven't been here, but listen to this: an 18th and 19th century collection of some professor and his son's embryological and anatomical specimens! Weird. It's out of the way in south-east Amsterdam and visits are by appointment only. Have a good time, I'm off to watch Frankenhooker again.

THE BIG ONES

For more information on the following museums pick up the free green "Amsterdam: City of Museums" pamphlet at the VVV. If you're here in the third week of april ask about Museum Weekend when all the big museums are free.

A Museum Card good for one year is available at all the big museums for ƒ45. This gets you in free or at a substantial discount to almost all the big ones mentioned below. If you're going to more than a few of these, or are returning within a year, then it's a good deal. You need one photo.

Rijksmuseum, Stadhouderskade 42, 673-2121
  Open tues-sat 10-17:00, sun 13-17:00. ƒ12.50, 18 and under ƒ5.

Vincent van Gogh Museum, Paulus Potterstraat 7, 570-5200
  Open tues-sat 10-17:00, sun 13-17:00. ƒ12.50.

Anne Frank House, Prinsengracht 263, 556-7100
  Open mon-sat 09-17:00, sun 10-17:00. Longer hours in summer. ƒ8, 17 and under ƒ4.50.

Stedelijk Museum, Paulus Potterstraat 13, 573-2911
  Open daily 11-17:00. ƒ8, 17 and under ƒ4.

Rembrandt House, Jodenbreestraat 4-6, 624-9486
  Open mon-sat 10-17:00, sun 13-17:00. ƒ7.50.

Amsterdam Historical Museum, Kalverstraat 92, 523-1822
  Open mon-fri 10-17:00, sat/sun 11-17:00. ƒ7.50, 16 and under ƒ3.75.

Jewish Historical Museum, J. Daniel Meyerplein 2-4, 626-9945
  Open daily 11-17:00. ƒ7, students ƒ3.50.

Under the Rijksmuseum.

WW2 Resistance Museum, Lekstraat 63, 644-9797
  Open tues-fri 10-17:00, sat/sun 13-17:00. ƒ4.50.

Maritime Museum, Kattenburgerplein 1, 523-2222
  Open tues-sat 10-17:00, sun 12-17:00, mondays in the summer 10-17:00.

Kröller-Müller Museum, Hoge Veluwe National Park.
  This is in the middle of Holland, but it has a huge and incredibly trippy sculpture garden and a fantastic collection of Van Gogh's. Free use of bikes on site. Should be experienced. Ask for details at the VVV.

MUSIC

Many guidebooks say that Amsterdam doesn't have a "world class" music scene, unlike some of its neighbouring capital cities. What a load of shit, but that shouldn't come as a surprise with a yuppie phrase like "world class". In fact, even if you're only here for a couple of days you should be able to find all kinds of music. From community run squats and old churches to dance halls and large clubs, this city is full of great venues and musicians.

HOW TO FIND OUT WHO'S PLAYING

A.U.B. - *Leidseplein 26, 621-1211*

The Amsterdams Uitburo (AUB) is the place to start a search into who's playing in Amsterdam. They have listings of all music happening in and around the city. Look on the counter for their flyer "Pop & Jazz Uitlijst". It has a regularly updated list of bands and venues in town. The A.U.B. also has flyers from the Paradiso and Sleepin-ARENA (see below) and lots of info on classical music, theatre and film. You can buy advance tickets here, but there's a ƒ2 service charge on each ticket. Open mon-sat 10-18:00 (thurs 'til 21:00).

Way Out Alternative Uitlijst

Someone is putting out this one page flyer every month. It includes listings for squat clubs and alternative movie theatres. Look for it in bars and in restaurants like the Egg Cream (see Restaurants, Food section).

To The Point

Tobacco companies kill people! Including the one that sponsors this flyer. (The one that sponsors the AUB uitlijst sucks, too). Having said that, this flyer is free, available in bars all over town and has english listings of bands, clubs and movie theatres.

Oor Magazine

The centre of this Dutch music magazine has a small insert that lists all the pop/rock shows coming to the Netherlands. It's a good source that is easily found in most bookstores.

Time Out Amsterdam

Two years ago *Time Out* magazine in London took over the production of Amsterdam's only decent english language magazine, formerly called *City Life Amsterdam*. They have a good day to day listing of all kinds of music, often with a short description of the band. It's available all over the city for ƒ5.

How to find out who's playing

Nieuwe Muziekhandel - *Leidsestraat 50, 623-7321*
In the window of this record store you'll find a frequently updated list of bands scheduled to play in Holland. There is also a ticket booth at the back of the store.

LIVE MUSIC/PARTY VENUES

Melkweg (Milkyway) - *Lijnsbaansgracht 234, 624-1777*
The Melkweg is located in a big warehouse (which used to be a dairy), on a canal just off Leidseplein. Although it's not the cheapest venue in town, there's so much to do inside that you get your money's worth. Shows range from ƒ10-ƒ25, depending of course on who's playing. In addition there is a membership fee of ƒ4 for a card that's good for one month. Most nights you'll find bands playing in the big hall. Also on the ground floor is an art gallery, and a bar/restaurant, (free entry to gallery from 14-17:00 mon and tues, 14-19:00 wed-sun). Explore the upstairs and you'll find a video room that's shows all different kinds of stuff from Annie Sprinkle and Sonic Youth to underground footage that you'd never find anywhere else. There is also live theatre, often in english, and a cinema (see Film section). Finally, at the very top is a mellow tea room. A complete listing is always available in front of the club.

Paradiso - *Weteringschans 6-8, 626-4521*
Located in a beautiful old church, this is an awesome place to see live music. There's a big dance floor with a balcony around it. Upstairs is a smaller hall where different bands sometimes jam after the main event. This is also a great venue for parties and performance art. I've seen everything from balloons filled with joints dropping from the ceiling to a live sex performance piece. Prince showed up not long ago and jammed all night! I love this place! A one month membership is ƒ4. If you're going to a sold out show it's a good idea to buy your membership in advance to avoid long line-ups.

Onafhankelijk Cultureel Centrum In It - *Amstelveenseweg 134, 671-7778*
This cool squat club has been here over 10 years. There's always something going on here: live music of all kinds, cabarets, readings, and other happenings. Their big hall has a bar, a nice sized stage and a big dance floor. Art pieces on display add to the hip atmosphere. Back by the entrance, an old stairway leads to the Kasbah café (see Bars section) on the second floor. Varied music and a fun, diverse crowd. Admission is usually ƒ5-10. Look for posters advertising events or wander by. This complex also houses a sauna (see Saunas, Hanging Out section). The building is located on the far side of Vondelpark, across the street and to the left. Tram 6.

PH 31 - *Prins Hendriklaan 31, 673-6850*

Located in the very classy area just south of Vondelpark is another long-established squat club called PH 31, after it's address. Live music happens mainly on tuesdays, wednesdays and thursdays. Wednesday's often consist of a jam session with a theme (ska, blues, groove, etc). I've seen some good punk bands here. Music starts at 22:00 and admission is ƒ5.

Casa Blanca - *Zeedijk 26, 625-5685*

Drinks at this tiny, cool jazz club are a bit expensive, but there is no cover except about once a month for special bookings. There's live music most nights and many musicians come to hang out and jam in this hip joint. Go man GO!

Sleepin-ARENA - *'s-Gravesandestraat 51, 694-7444*

The programming keeps getting better and better at the Sleep-In (see Places To Sleep section). They present all types of music here from disco to reggae to hard-core. The 400 capacity hall is roomy and comfortable: space to dance and space to watch. Guests staying here get a discount. Every friday is Underground Dance World. Average admission is ƒ10-15.

De Kroeg - *Lijnbaansgracht 163, 420-0232*

This small club has live music almost every night. Some nights, usually weekends, there's a cover charge. The front bar is relaxed and noisy and an easy place to meet people if the band is shit. Walk to the back and through the doors to reach a second bar and the stage. Don't be shy to push your way to the front: there's more room there. The music changes nightly: blues, jazz, rock, reggae, and sometimes open jam sessions. Listings are outside the club and posted around town.

Akhnaton - *Nieuwezijds Kolk 25, 624-3396*

This small club is a bit upscale and definitely a pick-up scene, but they have great music from Africa, usually on saturday nights. There are also Latin American and Asian music nights. The crowd consists mostly of smart dressers, but the good music always draws in a few grungy people like me. ƒ15.

Graan Silo - *Westerdoksdijk 51*

Every first saturday of the month is a World Music Evening for ƒ8. There's music, food and drink, and performances beginning about 21:30. Show up for a drink and to make your dinner reservation at 18:00. You can also come here for full meals on tue, fri and sunday (see Restaurants, Food section). Sometimes this amazing squat hosts artists' evenings of diverse performances. Music, poetry, films and slides, all occur at irregular intervals throughout the night. Drinks and delicious snacks are available at cheap, squat prices. Look for flyers listing dates. Bus 35, night bus 78.

Live music/party venues

Silo Drome Skate Party - *New Silo, Westerdoksdijk 51, 686-4322*
Different D.J.s spin their stuff here every thursday night and the disco tunes are perfect for a night of roller and inline skating. The passages in this subterranean maze are lit with coloured lights, slides and videos. The pillars are padded, which is lucky because running into them is how I usually stop. There's a really good mix of people: beginners, zoomers, dancers, kids. And a bar. And food. And couches and chairs where you can watch. Bring your own skates or go early and rent, ƒ5 for 1 hour, ƒ10 for 2 1/2 hours. Entrance ƒ5. Open 20-03:00. Bus 35, night bus 78.

Mystèr 2000 - *Lijnbaansgracht 92, 620-2970*
Located on a canal in the Jordaan, this is Amsterdam's first multimedia cybercentre. Inside this old textile factory you'll find a smart bar, performance spaces, a studio, a library and more. Wednesday nights at 21:00 are set aside for music and poetry. Every thursday at 17:00 they host an Internet Café where you can "surf" on one of the dozen computer terminals, or attend an Internet Workshop for beginners (ƒ30). Come at 18:00 on friday for the Brain Saloon (ƒ5) and experience a 15 minute session on a brain machine or try a smart drink. On the last sunday of every month is the cool Bazaar Attitude (see Markets, Shopping section). Stop in and pick up a flyer for a complete rundown of everything else offered at Mystèr 2000, including: performances, theatre, changing exhibitions, and courses in yoga, meditation, massage, and music. Travellers can pick-up or send E-mail for ƒ10/hour, (mystèr@net.info.nl). Open tues-sun 11-17:00.

Inrichting Alternative Dance Night - *New Silo, Westerdoksdijk 51*
This is the latest home for this bi-monthly gathering of goths, vampires and everyone else who likes to dress all in black when they go out dancing. The organisers have been presenting these events for over three years now and they go out of their way to create a genuinely gothic environment. There are often live performances, and down in the pit is another bar and chill-out space. Open 22-04:00 every second saturday of the month. Admission ƒ4 plus membership. Bus 35, night bus 78.

Apocalypse Alternative Dance Party - *Goliath, Beyersweg 28*
Even though this isn't a live music event you should go if you like dancing to punk, gothic, wave, industrial and other interesting, alternative music. Most of the crowd from the Inrichting (see above) will be there and the Goliath, with it's high ceilings, woodwork, and fireplace is perfect for this kind of event. This is an occasional thing, so look for flyers around town advertising the next one. Entrance ƒ5 and drinks are cheap. Tram 9, night bus 71.

Mono Café - *Oude Zijds Voorburgwal 2, 625-3630*
Local bands often play here on friday and saturday nights. Sixties style garage and punk are on the menu. Every thursday night a d.j. spins tunes for a "Wild Sixties Surf Special". This is also a cool spot in the day, (see Cafés section). Bands start about 22:00. Open sun-thurs 10-01:00, fri/sat 10-02:00.

DANCE CLUBS

If you're into dance clubs, raves, parties, etc. get a copy of *Time Out Amsterdam* magazine. Or refer back to Club Fashions in the Shopping section: those stores all have party information. Here is a list of some of the discos and clubs in the city.

De Trut - *Bilderdijkstraat 156*
Sunday night this basement squat club comes alive with a gay disco that draws a crazy, mixed crowd. Admission is only ƒ1! Doors close at 23:30 and the queens dance until dawn.

Tempel - *Herengracht 114, 622-7685*
Located in an old canal house. Hosts lots of parties and theme evenings featuring all kinds of music.

Mazzo - *Rozengracht 114, 626-7500*
Relaxed. Daily 'til 04/05:00. Call first; they just had a fire!

Soul Kitchen - *Amstelstraat 32, 620-2333*
Disco, soul.

It - *Amstelstraat 24, 625-0111*
Trendy gay disco (mixed crowd, except on sat). Good window displays outside. Good people-watching inside. 23-04/05:00.

Cockring - *Warmoesstraat 96, 623-9604*
Male only. 23-04/05:00.

Club 216 - *Oude Zijds Voorburgwal 216, 627-1977*
Shit place. Shit staff. Thurs-sat 22-05:00.

Roxy - *Singel 465, 620-0354*
Trendy. Dress code and membership. Wed night gay. 23-04/05:00.

Richter - *Reguliersdwarsstraat 36, 626-1573*
Trendy. Dress code and membership. 23-04/05:00.

Street music

Escape - *Rembrandtplein 11, 622-3542*
  Very hot at the moment. 22-04/05:00.

Dansen bij Jansen - *Handboogstraat 11, 620-1779*
  Students. 23-04/05:00.

Odeon - *Singel 460, 624-9711*
  Lots of students. 3 floors. 23-05:00.

Marcanti Plaza - *Jan Van Galenstraat 6-10, 682-3456*
  Big dance club on sat. 23-05:00.

Seymour Likely 2 - *Nieuwezijds Voorburgwal 161, 420-5062*
  Trendy. I've never been here. 24:00-?

STREET MUSIC

Take a walk around Amsterdam on any warm day (and some cold ones!) and you'll find street musicians everywhere. Popular areas for people to play include Dam square, Leidsestraat and Leidseplein, Vondelpark (which also has a big stage in the summer) and Central Station. If I stop and listen for awhile I always give a guilder or two, which I think is a pretty good deal for having someone liven up the streets and people of a city.

RADIO

Radio 100 - *98.2FM*
  This pirate radio station has been around a long time. They have a wide range of shows covering many subjects and all types of music. They play an outstanding selection of music from around the world.

Radio Patapoe - *101.5FM*
  Power to the pirates. Diverse programming since 1989, featuring all kinds of cool music. All with no commercials. Yes!

BBC World Service - *648AM*
  Various shows, but best of all news in english every hour on the hour (except 20:00 when it's in German). French news at 18:30.

MVS - *106.8FM/103.8FM cable*
  This is a gay operated station. Music, news, interviews, etc. are broadcast in english on sundays from 18-20:00.

Radio de Vrije Keizer - *96.2FM*

More old-timers on the pirate scene who became famous for their diverse, sometimes crazy programming of everything from politics to poop.

World Radio Network - *97FM*

News from national radio stations all over the world, many in english.

FESTIVALS

All summer long there are festivals happening in and around Amsterdam. The ones that I've listed are free except for the African Music Festival and Parade. For any without precise dates, check with the VVV.

Anti-Racism Demo - *Third week of March*

This enormous, annual march through Amsterdam draws huge crowds (50-70,000 people) to celebrate the international day of protest against racism (March 21). All kinds of people hit the streets for a day of singing, dancing, and chanting that culminates in a lively fair. Look for posters or call the organisers at 676-6710 for details.

Queen's Day - *30 April (29 April in '95), Everywhere in Holland*

The biggest and best party of the year happens on this day. Amsterdam becomes one big carnival, with music and dancing and gallivanting and carousing. The world's biggest flea market opens for business: anything can be bought or sold. The celebrations start the night before and last 24 hours. It's unbelievably fun.

Bevrijdingsdag - *05 May, Various locations, Amsterdam*

This one celebrates Holland's liberation from the Nazis at the end of WW2: something worth celebrating. This year will be extra big because it's the 50th anniversary, and the festivities will be taking place in Dam Square and on stages along Rokin. If you're interested in seeing some of Holland's bigger bands, check this out. It's always a fun party. Fuck Nazis!

Park Pop - *25 June 1995, Zuiderpark, Den Haag*

This is the 15th year of Europe's biggest free (which is why I mention it here even though it's not in Amsterdam) pop festival and thousands of people will be there. Every year sees an interesting line-up of performers playing all kinds of music. It's definitely worth trucking out to The Hague for this one.

Festivals

Rendez Vous - *Mid-end July, Amsterdam*

This will be the fourth year for this big AIDS fund-raiser. Dozens of bands play on the outdoor stage during the week-long event. The music is free, but you'd be an asshole not to give a donation. Check with the VVV for the location this year.

African Music Festival - *Early Aug, DHC Stadion, Delft*

Here is another festival that's outside of Amsterdam. This incredible feast of African music gets better every year. Some of Africa's best and most famous stars play here, in a big field outside of Delft. Tickets are usually ƒ30. Camping isn't allowed, but trains run back to Amsterdam all night.

Parade - *Mid August, Martin Luther King Park*

This old-style European carnival is produced by the same trippy people who did the Boulevard of Broken Dreams several years ago. As the sun goes down on the circle of tents, barkers and performers compete to draw you inside, where you'll witness strange, otherworldly spectacles that defy the imagination. It's really something special. Admission is about ƒ6 and, once inside, some of the attractions also charge an admission fee.

Uitmarkt - *End August, Various locations, Amsterdam*

To celebrate the beginning of the new cultural season, Amsterdam's streets become full of theatre, dance, and live music. All for free.

Cannabis Cup Awards - *Third week november, Amsterdam*

High Times magazine has hosted this marijuana festival seven times, and it's getting bigger every year. Several days of celebrations centred around cannabis culminate in the actual awards given for the best strains of grass. It's mainly an amerikan affair, but each year sees more of an international flavour seeping in. Except for the awards party, most of the events, like the hemp expo and fashion show, are free.

"Fashion Show" at a squatters' street festival. (Photo: Elsbeth Gugger)

Highlife Cup - *Beginning of december, Amsterdam*
For more info call 041 04 98 112

This harvest festival is really a Dutch affair, although last year they opened it up to other European growers. *Highlife* magazine organises the awards and the big party where they are given away. They have speakers, live music, and plenty to smoke! Call for details.

BARS

Vrankrijk - *Spuistraat 216 (1)*
Even if this established squat bar didn't have a sign you'd have no trouble finding it thanks to the building's wild paint job. Go late if you want to be in a crowd. Buzz to get inside. There you'll find a high ceilinged room covered with political posters, and heated (in winter) by a big, friendly wood burning stove. Despite all the punks hanging around, they play all kinds of music. Occasionally they have bands, performances and slide shows. The Vrankrijk is one of the cheapest bars in the city: beer ƒ1.75, juice ƒ1. Upstairs in the back there's lots of anarchist literature. Open weekdays 22-02:00, weekends 'til 03:00.

Café the Minds - *Spuistraat 245, 623-6784 (2)*

This is a comfortably run down bar with a lot of character. It's located not far from the Vrankrijk. They have a pool table (only ƒ1!) and a pinball machine and they play good grunge and rock and metal. It's a fun place to hang out and have a drink while you decide where to go next.

Café Weber - *Marnixstraat 397 (3)*

When you walk in here it looks like a nice, ordinary, Amsterdam "brown" café. But downstairs you'll find a cool basement room decked out with old couches, big armchairs, lots of candles and a little greenhouse. It's a great place to sit around with some friends, even if the beer is a bit overpriced. It's location close to Leidseplein is a plus. Open sun-thurs 20-02:00, fri/sat 20:00-03:00.

Soundgarden - *Marnixstraat 164-166, 620-2853 (4)*

The giant photo of Iggy that greets you here sets the tone for music that's loud and grungy, much to the appreciation of the leather-clad dudes and chicks that hang here. Actually, a lot of different people come in for a night of pool, darts and pinball. Also, the terrace over the water out back is a great spot in the summer to smoke a joint and have a drink. Open sun-thurs 13-01:00, fri/sat 13-02:00.

Brouwerij 't IJ - *Funenkade 7 (5)*

For those of you who are here for a short time, here's your chance to do two tourist essentials at once: drink a Dutch beer other than Heineken and see a windmill. The brewery in this beautiful, old mill sells its draft (with alcohol content up to 9 percent!) to an appreciative crowd of regulars in its smoky, noisy pub. On sunny days the terrace is packed, but there's always one more spot on the ground. It's a bit out of the centre, not far from the Dappermarkt (see Markets, Shopping section) and the Tropenmuseum (see Museums section). Open wed-sun 15-20:00.

Kasbah - *Amstelveenseweg 134*

This is a happening squat café in the same beautiful building as the Cultureel Centrum In It (see Live Venues, Music section). Its one room is fixed up with plants and old tables with candles on them. Artwork and posters hang from the ceiling and walls, and fanzines are scattered about. It's good place to find info on performances and political events around Amsterdam. Drinks are cheap cheap CHEAP! A big glass of apple juice (my poison) is ƒ1. Bottled beer starts at ƒ1.75.

Korsakoff - *Lijnbaansgracht 161, 625-7874 (6)*

This club used to be famous for its hard-core nights. Now it's got a sound system playing a mix of music: hip hop, industrial, sometimes punk. The decor and artwork is interesting and changes often. Upstairs is another bar and a pool table. Some nights it's really fun with a lively, dancing crowd; other nights... dead. Buzz to get in. Open 22-02:00, weekends 'til 03:00.

Queers In Space - *Westermarkt 7, 420-6267 (7)*

Queer punks don't have The Dirk anymore (R.I.P.) thanks to shit-for-brains banks and politicians. But don't worry because now there's Queers in Space! Once a week all you juvenile delinquents can get together at this small squat right across the street from the Homomonument. Mixed music and mixed crowd. Have fun kids. Open every saturday from 13-19:00. Free.

Squat art protesting the plans of ABN-AMRO bank to build a huge, hideous shopping/ parking/ office/ luxury appartment complex in place of dozens of beautiful, old buildings (see garbage can). The squatters have since been evicted and the houses demolished.

Café Sas - *Marnixstraat 79, 420-4075 (8)*

Walk into this café at the north end of the Marnixstraat and you can tell immediately that it's an artists' haunt. Regulars have produced paintings, sculptures and other artwork to create a cluttered, comfortable environment. Candles add to this relaxing atmosphere and in the back are a couch, some easy chairs and a canal view. During the day they serve cakes and sandwiches from ƒ3.50, and soup of the day for ƒ5. At night food is available in the restaurant downstairs. On weekends they often have live music and the place is packed. Open mon-thurs 13-01:00, fri/sat 13-02:00.

De Buurvrouw - *St Pieterpoortsteeg 29, 625-9654 (10)*

Occasionally you can catch some live music here, but mainly it's just a cool spot to hang out and have a drink. I like the fact that it's on a little alley. It makes it a bit difficult to find; that and the slightly twisted artwork, lends it an underground feel. Open sun-thurs 20-02:00, fri/sat 21-03:00.

'T Smackzeyl - *Brouwersgracht101, 622-6520 (11)*
A traditional Amsterdam "brown" café with high ceilings and big windows overlooking two of the most beautiful canals - the Brouwersgracht and the Prinsengracht. In nice weather customers bring stools out to the sidewalk to watch the sunset. Open sun-thurs 11-01:00, fri/sat 11-02:00.

De Duivel (The Devil) - *Reguliersdwarsstraat 87, 626-6184 (12)*
Finally, a cool place playing hip-hop and rap on a regular basis! Friday nights have live music and sunday nights are also hip. Come check out the locals doing their turntable/mike thing. Peace to all the tourists, cuz I got a lotta love. Open sun-thurs 20-02:00, fri/sat 20-03:00.

The Itonia - *Kloveniersburgwal 20 (13)*
This squatted building is right across from a police station. HA! Once a week there is an open stage where anything can happen - plays, readings, singing, etc. - based on a theme thought up the week before. During the break members of the audience head out on the streets with a video camera for some guerrilla film-making, the results of which are shown when they return. The whole thing is a lot of fun and mainly in English. The place is very small though and fills up early, so don't be upset if you don't get in. It's not because you're a nerd (or they wouldn't have let me in). Open wednesdays from 22:00.

De Koe (The Cow) - *Marnixstraat 381, 625-4482 (14)*
One of Amsterdam's newer cafés is divided into two sections. Upstairs is a roomy bar that serves snacks and sandwiches. Bands play live every sunday from 16-18:00. On weekdays, it's a mellow place to go and hear some blues if you want to escape from from the crowds of nearby Leidseplein. Downstairs after 18:00 you can eat daily specials from ƒ13. Open sun-thurs 11-01:00, fri/sat 13-02:00.

Du Lac - *Haarlemmerstraat 118, 624-4265 (15)*
This place has lots of little rooms and corners to sit in with large or small groups of friends. Their attempt at "zany" decor doesn't quite work, yet it's still a lively place to have a drink. There's a garden in the back and sometimes they feature live music on sunday afternoons. Beer is a bit pricey at ƒ3. Open mon-thurs 16-01:00, fri/sat 16-02:00, sun 14-01:00.

Jan Steen Bar - *Ruysdaelkade 149 (16)*
This old bar is pretty nice, but I mention it here primarily for it's cheap prices: draft beer ƒ1.75 and most shots ƒ3.50. Located out near the Albert Cuyp market.

FILM

The great thing about being a visitor to Amsterdam and seeing a movie is that the Dutch never dub films. They are always shown in their original language with Dutch subtitles. The big first-run theatres are centred mostly around Leidseplein and are expensive: usually ƒ13-ƒ15 on weekends. A recent introduction to the big theatres is reduced rates for off-peak showings. Matinees from mon-fri are only ƒ8.50. Weekday evenings and weekend matinees are ƒ11. Some longer movies may cost more, so always ask the price.

The bad thing about being a visitor to Amsterdam and seeing a movie is the stupid, fucking "pauze" in the middle of every film. Presumably this 15 minute break is a big money maker for the theatres as everyone files out to buy beer, coffee, and junk food. What it really is though, is an abrupt, unwelcome interruption of the film that never fails to come at the worst moment. Don't say I didn't warn you.

For a listing of films pick up "De Week Agenda", a free weekly agenda of films and other events around Amsterdam. It comes out every thursday and is available in bars, restaurants and theatres.

Riksbioscoop - *Back of Tuschinski Theatre. Entrance on Reguliersdwarsstr.*

This is the best deal in the city, even if most of the films are 1-2 year old Hollywood hits. The price is only ƒ2.50 and the film changes every thursday. I remember the good old days when the place used to be empty all the time, but now it's gotten very popular, so buy your tickets early. One woman in the ticket booth is a real bitch.

Tuschinski - *Reguliersbreestraat 26-28, 626-2633*

This art-deco theatre was built in 1922 and it might be the most beautiful movie theatre anywhere. Although it's expensive, it's worth the price to see a film in the main hall (theatre #1). Go early so you have time to look at the ornate lobby/café. This is where the queen goes to see movies.

Nederlands Film Museum - *Vondelpark 3, 589-1400*

This museum/cinema/café is situated in a big old mansion in Vondelpark. They have two or three different films every day, usually for ƒ8.50, but sometimes cheaper. You can pick up a monthly listing in the lobby. It's in Dutch, but check where the film was made, because they show many from the US and Britain. The two small theatres here show everything from old B+W classics, to rock 'n roll films, to cult slashers. The café is also very nice (see Vertigo, Café section).

Desmet - *Plantage Middenlaan 4A, 627-3434*

This is a beautiful art-deco theatre with a great program that has no commercials and no pauze! Sun-wed is cheaper at ƒ10. Thurs-sat ƒ14. They have interesting late night shows and a gay film series. And like all good alternative movie houses, they have a café in the lobby. Go early to look at the changing photo exhibits (once there were shots of Pasolini in the nude!).

Filmhuis Cavia - *Van Hallstraat 52-1, 684-8239*

This little cinema lies just west of the city centre over a boxing club. Its rep programme runs every wednesday and thursday. Bottled beer in their café is only ƒ1.75 and admission is a very reasonable ƒ6. Films start at 21:00.

Kriterion - *Roeterstraat 170, 623-1708*

This recently renovated art-house theatre is not too far from the Sleepin. They usually have an interesting program and there's also a relaxed, busy café in the lobby. Sun-thurs ƒ10, fri/sat ƒ12.

Soeterijn - *Linneausstraat 2, 568-8252*

This theatre, attached to the Tropenmuseum, isn't the nicest, but rarely shown films from around the world are screened here, for example a series of comedies from Iran and Egypt. Call to find out if the subtitles are in english. ƒ10.

The Movies - *Haarlemmerdijk 161, 638-6016*

There's usually at least one second-run US or British film playing in this small theatre, but it's expensive (ƒ13.50). The lobby is beautiful and sometimes there's live music!

Cereal Killah Sundays - *C.I.A., Droogbak 2-1, 627-1646*

Every sunday afternoon you can join a bunch of amerikan ex-pats eating crap like Cap'n Crunch, Fruity Pebbles (and a myriad of other glow-in-the-dark cereals), while watching cartoons and a feature horror movie on video. Cereals cost 7 to 10 cents a gram, which works out to an average of ƒ3.60 a bowl. Admission, milk and coffee are free. Drop by about 15:00.

Cult Videotheek - *Amstel 47, 622-7843*

The Cool Guide To Amsterdam wouldn't be complete without the coolest video store in Amsterdam. Their impressive selection includes foreign films, sexploitation, cult and trash, and a lot more. They even have *No Skin Off My Ass* by Bruce LaBruce. Occasionally, there are second hand videos for sale. As a tourist you probably won't go there, but if you decide to move to Amsterdam and have a video machine, give me a call my friend! Open daily 13-21:00.

SEX

Sex and lots of it: it's a big part of tourism in Amsterdam. The Red Light District is always crowded and colourful, not to mention sleazy. It's located in the neighbourhood just south-east of Central Station. You'll find streets and alleyways lined with sex shops, live sex shows, and rows and rows of red lights illuminating the windows of Amsterdam's famous prostitutes. This area is pretty safe, but women alone sometimes get hassled and may want to tour this part of town in the daytime. Everyone should watch out for pickpockets.

There is also a smaller Red Light area around the Spuistraat and the Singel Canal at the Central Station end. And another one, frequented mainly by Dutch men, runs along the Ruysdaelkade by Albert Cuypstraat. While the Red Light Districts are concentrated in these areas, several of the places I recommend are in other parts of the city.

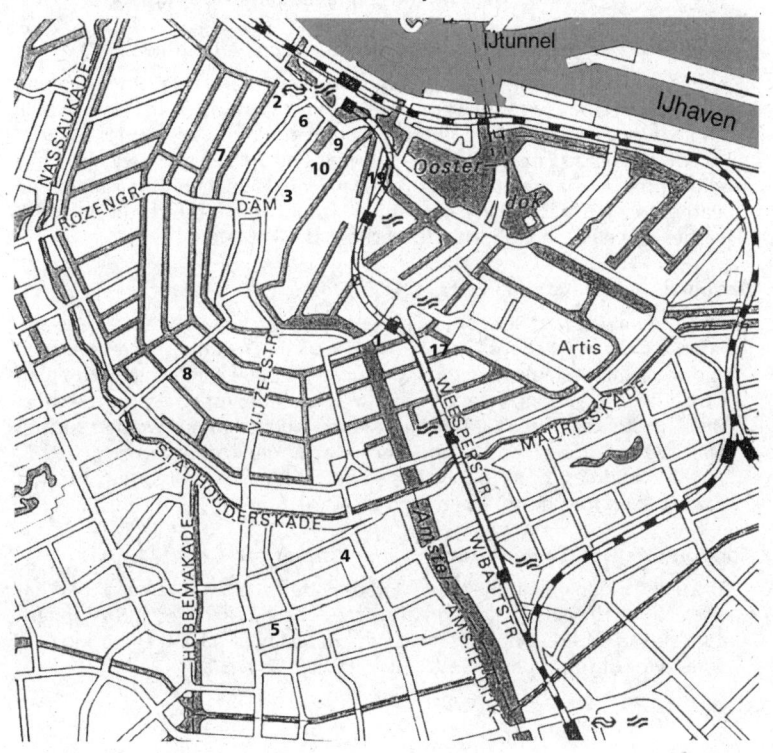

If you're interested in finding out more about prostitution in Holland, stop in at the Prostitution Information Centre (see below), and pick up a copy of the *Pleasure Guide*. It's full of interesting and educational news, facts, and stories. It's only ƒ3.25 and it's in dutch and english.

In case you were wondering, the services of a prostitute in the Red Light District start at ƒ50 for a blow-job and ƒ50 for a fuck. That price gives you about 15-20 minutes. The condom is included free of charge.

SEX SHOPS

You'll find them every twenty metres in the Red Light District and you should definitely take a peek inside one. These places all carry roughly the same selection of sex toys, magazines and videos, ranging from really funny to seriously sexy to disgusting. If you're going to do a little shopping remember that most of the cheap stuff is of poor quality and you get what you pay for. For better quality I'd recommend the following shop:

Female and Partners - *Amstel 47 (near Waterlooplein), 620-9152 (1)*

This is the coolest and classiest sex shop in Amsterdam. It's women-run and offers an alternative to the very male dominated sex industry. Inside you'll find a select, wide range of vibrators, dildos and other sex articles. They've recently expanded their selection of books and videos, and they also have some incredibly sexy clothes that you won't find elsewhere. The rubber and leather wear is particularly impressive! Stop in for information on fetish parties as well. Open mon 13-18:00, tues-sat 11-18:00.

Absolute Danny - *Stromarkt 13, 421-0915 (2)*

Amsterdam's newest sex shop is also woman-run and you can tell the difference from other shops as soon as you walk in. The atmosphere is relaxed and welcoming: single women and couples will feel comfortable shopping here. The owner, Danny, designs a lot of the clothes especially for the shop. She also stocks erotic literature and books about famous women such as Mae West, Brigitte Bardot, and Betty Page. You'll find sex toys, videos, artwork, and best of all, penis-shaped pasta! It makes a great gift for that hard to shop for person. Open mon 13-18:00, tues-sat 11-18:00.

Condomerie Het Gulden Vlies - *Warmoesstraat 141, 627-4174 (3)*

The first condomerie in the world and definitely the best I've been to. What a selection! They also have a great display of condom boxes and wrappers. It's a very laid-back shop that makes the necessity of buying and using condoms a lot of fun. Open mon-fri 13-18:00, sat 12-17:30.

Nolly's Sexboetiek - *Sarphatipark 99, 673-4767 (4)*

In the back of this shop I found a bunch of dusty gay and straight super 8 and 8mm films from the 60's and 70's for only about ƒ10. I don't have a projector, but this could be a real find for collectors and I thought you might be interested. Nolly also has a big selection of magazines, some that I didn't see in the Red Light District. Call for hours.

Blue and White - *Ceintuurbaan 248, 610-1741 (5)*

This is another sex shop in the neighbourhood of the Albert Cuyp Market (see Markets, Shopping section). They have all the required stuff plus a bargain bin full of dildos and other toys, discount videos, and European editions of Penthouse and Playboy for ƒ3.95. Open sun-fri 09:30-18:00 (thurs 'til 21:00), sat 12-17:00.

Alpha Blue - *Nieuwendijk 26, 627-1664 (6)*

I don't know, but I've been told, the cheapest condoms, here are sold. Apparently videos are cheaper here than in the Red Light District too. You can spot this place by the life-size Betty Page cut-out in front. Remember that videos are on a different system here than in North America. Open daily 09-01:00.

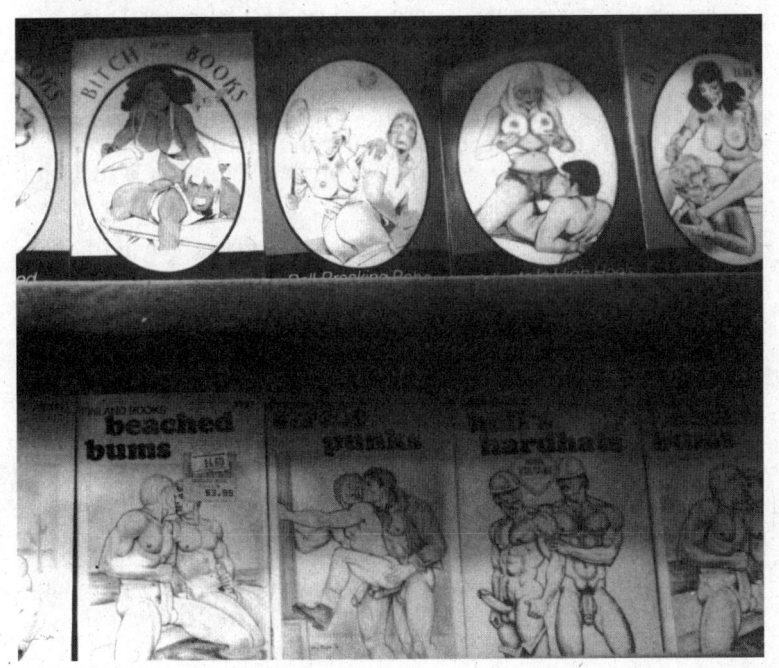

NVSH - *Blauburgwal 7-9, 623-9359 (7)*
The window of this sex shop/information centre always looks so inviting that I wasn't prepared for the cold, clinical atmosphere inside. In fact, the only reason I'm mentioning this place is because of the theme evenings that some of you might enjoy: transvestite and transsexual evenings, exhibitionism nights, erotic massage for couples, and more. Call for times, prices and reservations. Doors close early and (I guess) the fun begins. Visitors to Amsterdam are welcome. Shop open mon-fri 11-18:00, sat 12-17:00.

The Bronx - *Kerkstraat 53-55, 623-1548 (8)*
This sex shop for gay men has an impressive collection of books, magazines and videos. There are also leather goods, sex toys and the biggest butt-plug I've ever seen! There's a cinema and in the back are some video cabins. If you get really worked up run across the street to "Thermos Night" (#58-60), where f22.50 gets you saunas, films, bars, and lots of sweaty guys. Bronx open daily 12-24:00.

PEEP SHOWS AND LIVE SEX

There are several peepshow places scattered around the Red Light District. I looked into one and this is what I peeped. In a telephone booth sized room I put a guilder in a slot and a little window went up. Lo and behold there was a young couple fucking on a revolving platform about two feet from my face. It wasn't very passionate, but they were definitely doing it. One guilder gets you 30 seconds. Then I went into a little sit-down booth and for another guilder I got 100 seconds of a video peepshow. There is a built-in channel changer and a choice of over 150 videos. Everything is there including bestiality and brown showers. The verdict? Well, I found it kind of interesting in a weird sort of way. There were mostly men peeping, obviously, but there were also two couples looking around. If you're curious, you should go take a look: nobody knows you here anyway.

In the name of research I also saw a few sex shows. At some you can bargain with the doorman, and the average admission price ends up being about f20-f25. Inside an appropriately sleazy little theatre women will strip to loud disco music. Sometimes they get someone from the audience to participate by removing lingerie or inserting a vibrator. Then a couple will have sex. It's very mechanical and not very exciting, but it will satisfy your curiosity. At other shows you pay a set price of f50 to sit in a clean, comfortable theatre and watch better looking strippers and couples. Again, it's not really sexy, but the show was more entertaining. I especially liked one couple who did a choreographed routine to Mozart's Requiem. It was very dramatic and the woman wore lots of leather and had several piercings!

MISCELLANEOUS SEX STUFF

G-Force (SM Café) - *Oudezijds Armsteeg 7, 420-1664 (9)*

G-Force is an SM friendly café in a little alley off the Warmoesstraat. The atmosphere inside is very open and relaxed. All kinds of drinks are served and lots of SM magazines are scattered around for you to peruse. They have changing displays of SM inspired artwork, and SM videos often playing in one corner. G-Force hosts several parties including: special info evenings for couples; "Female Fortress" for women only; youth nights for people up to 25 years old; "Power Party" for men under 36, and more. Every thursday is fetish night with no admission charge, but there is a strict dress code. Behind the bar is a trap door leading down to a well equipped dungeon. Everything you could ever want or need is there, including some specially designed masks and "machinery". The dungeon can be rented for private use for f100/hour. Don't go here if you're turned off by the scene, but if you're curious, you will be very welcome. Open daily 14-24:00.

G-force also publishes a monthly agenda listing events they host as well as other fetish parties around the city. It only costs ƒ1 and is available at the café.

Hellen's Place (woman-friendly erotic café) - *Overtoom 497, 689-5501*

Was I ever surprised last summer when I went to check on the all-you-can-eat rib place that used to be here and found instead an erotic café! Everyone is welcome: singles, couples, dykes, fags, fetishists, exhibitionists, transsexuals, and anyone who's just curious. There is a bar with normal priced drinks, a stage, and changing erotic exhibitions. In Hellen's words, "we provide the opportunity and the atmosphere, the visitors make the party". Anything goes except obtrusive behaviour. In the basement is an erotic play area. There you'll find a darkroom (mixed!), a continuous peep-show, SM facilities and more. Entrance is ƒ5 on weeknights, ƒ7.50 on fri/sat. Students half price! Entrance to the play area is another ƒ5 and is for members only (you'll have to ask about membership). Open sun-thurs 20-03:00, fri/sat 20-04:00.

Fetish Faction - *Catacomb Studio, Haarlemmerstraat 124c, 697-8094*

Those into leather, rubber, plastic, etc, will enjoy these little get-togethers, which are a bit more intimate than some of the other fetish parties happening now. There is a playroom, an SM room and, of course, dancing. Admission varies. Strict fetish dress code. Call for details. For info on other fetish parties check out Demask at Zeedijk 64, Wrapped at Singel 434, or Female and Partners (see above).

Prostitution Information Centre (PIC) - *Enge Kerksteeg 3, 420-7328 (10)*

The PIC was established last august. They offer advice and information about prostitution in the Netherlands to tourists, prostitutes, their clients, and anyone else who's interested. It's located in the heart of the Red Light District and is open to the public. Inside you'll find pamphlets, flyers, and books about all aspects of prostitution. The woman who runs the centre also gives a six week course in how to be a prostitute. The course, (in dutch), covers such topics as history, health, and taxes, and is for both men and women. There is also a course in striptease! Call for hours.

Amsterdam Call Girls - *600-2354*

This fully legal (registered at the chamber of commerce!) escort service is owned and co-operatively run by women. they've been around for just over 4 years and have an excellent reputation. If you have the money (it's very expensive) and go in for this sort of thing, these are the ones you should be supporting: women who have taken control of their chosen profession and, as a result, are making their lives and those of their colleagues healthier and safer.

A Note About Prostitution

The decriminalisation of prostitution in Holland is one step in a long, slow process of public recognition and acceptance by the Dutch people of the commercial sale of sex in their midst. Under Dutch law prostitutes are regarded as victims and only pimps and organisers risk prosecution. However, as with the laws concerning soft drugs, these are not enforced. Because prostitution in the Netherlands has not been forced underground it is one of the safest places in the world for sex-trade workers and their clients to do business.

In spite of this progressive legal climate however, sex-trade workers remain socially stigmatised and are still often exploited. Many of them lead a double life and this is one of the reasons they have such a strong aversion to being photographed. (Don't do it: you're asking for trouble.)

Prostitutes in the Netherlands are not required by law to undergo STD testing. This situation is strongly supported by the prostitutes union (The Red Thread) and members of the women's movement who work to ensure the human rights of sex-trade workers.

DICTIONARY

Note: "g" is pronounced like a low growl, like the noise you make when you try to scratch an itch at the back of your throat, like the ch in Chanukah. I'll use "gh" in my attempt at the phonetic spellings. Good luck (you'll need it).

hello/goodbye	= dag (dagh)		rice/noodles	= nasi/bami (in indonesian restaurants)
see ya	= tot ziens (tote zeens)		cosy	= gezellig (ghezeligh)
thank you	= dank je wel/bedankt (dahnk ye vel /bidahnkt)		what a drag	= wat jammer (vhat yahmmer)
you're welcome/ please	= alsjeblieft (allsh-yuhbleeft)		cheers	= proost
			watch out	= pas op
fuck off	= rot op		squat	= kraakpand (krahk pahnt)
do you speak english?	= spreek je engels? (spreyk ye eyngels)		fag	= nichtje (nichtchye)
how much does that cost?	= hoe veel kost dat? (hoo feyl cost dat)		dykes	= potten
			bicycle	= fiets (feets)
stoned as a shrimp	= stoned als een garnaal		links	= left
			rechts	= right
got a light?	= vuurtje? (foortchye)		1	= een (eyn)
			2	= twee (tvey)
toke	= blow		3	= drie (dree)
to blowjob	= pijpen (pie-pen)		4	= vier (feer)
store	= winkel (veenkel)		5	= vijf (fiyf)
delicious	= lekker		6	= zes (zes)
food, to eat, meal	= eten (eyten)		7	= zeven (zeven)
			8	= acht (ahcht)
			9	= negen (nayghen)
			10	= tien (teen)

PHONE NUMBERS
EMERGENCY AND HEALTH

Emergency (police, ambulance, fire) 06-11

Police (non-emergency) 559-9111

First Aid (OLVG Hospital, 1st Oosterparkstraat 179) 599-9111

Sexual Assault Help Line (24 hours) 612-7576

Anti-Discriminatie Bureau (complaints about fascism and racism) 638-5551

Doctors Service (24 hours) 664-2111; (days) 624-5793; (nights) 612-3766

Health Clinic (Gezondheidswinkel De Witte Jas, de Wittenstraat 29) 688-1140

Travellers Vaccination Clinic (GG & GD, Nieuwe Achtergracht 100; 08-10:00) 555-5370

Dental Emergencies (24 hours) 06 821-2230

ACTA Dental clinic (mon-fri 09-10:00;13:30-14:30) 518-8888

Pharmacies Info Line (includes after-hours locations; message is in Dutch) 694-8709

Aids Hotline (personal info and consultation about aids; mon-fri 14-22:00) 06 022-2220

VD Clinic (free and anonymous treatment; Groenburgwal 44; mon-fri 08-10:30 or by appt.) 555-5822

Birth Control Clinic (Aletta Jacobshuis, Overtoom 323; 09-16:30) 616-6222

Women's Health Centre (tues 09-12:00, thurs 19-22:00, fri 13-16:00) 693-4358

Abortion Clinics: MR'70 624-5426; Polikliniek Oosterpark 693-2151

Free Legal Advice 548-2611; 626-4477

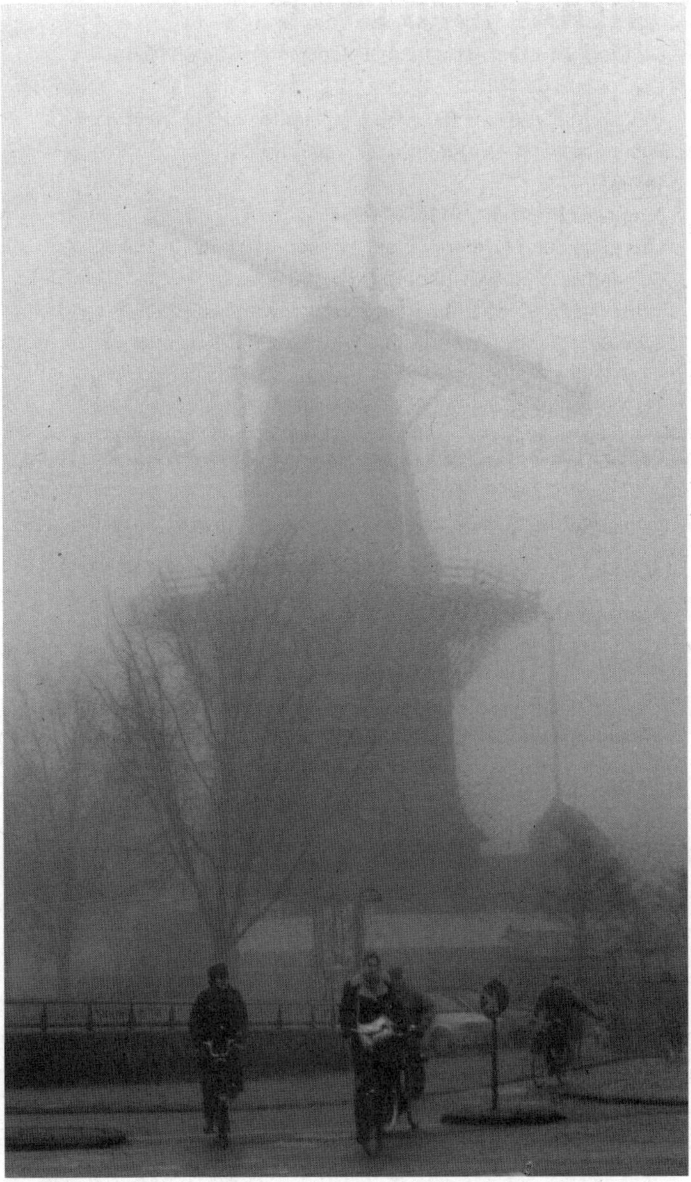

GENERAL INFO LINES

Directory Assistance: Holland 06-8008; International 06-0418
Collect calls 06-0410
VVV Tourist Info Line (50 cents per minute) 06-340-34066
Public Transport & International Train Info (50 cents per minute) 06-9292
Taxi 677-7777
Schiphol Airport 601-9111; 601-0966
Lost and Found (Waterlooplein 11; mon-fri 11-15:30) 559-8005
Gay and Lesbian Switchboard (info and advice; 10-22:00) 623-6565
Youth Advice Centre (assistance to run-aways) 624-2949
Women's Centre (Vrouwenhuis Amsterdam, Nieuwe Herengracht 95; café open wed & thurs 11-16:00) 625-2066

EMBASSIES AND CONSULATES

(070 = Den Haag/ 010 = Rotterdam)

Amerika 664-5661
Australia 070 310-8200
Austria 626-8033
Belgium 6429763
Britain 676-4343
Canada 070 364-4825
Czech 575-3016
Denmark 682-9991
Egypt 070 354-2000
Finland 624-9090
France 624-8346
Germany 673-6245
Greece 624-3671
Hungary 070 350-0404
India 070 346-9771
Ireland 070 363-0993
Israel 070 364-7850
Italy 624-0043
Luxembourg 301-5555
Morocco 070 346-9617
New Zealand/ Aotearoa 070 346-7850
Norway 624-2331
Poland 070 360-2806
Portugal 010 411-1540
Spain 620-3811
Sweden 682-2111
Switzerland 664-4231
Thailand 679-9916
Turkey 070 360 4912

Winner High Times Cup

1994   **1995**

Green House

TOLSTRAAT

WATERLOOPLEIN

CAFÉ - COFFEESHOP
Amsterdam

Tolstraat 91 (hoek v. Woustr.)   Waterlooplein 345
Tel. 020-6737430   Tel. 020-6225499

Info: 06-8898.1280

WHERE EAST MEETS WEST

Raves from the critics for this book

"Where DID the author dig up this pack of lies? Amsterdam is NOT, I repeat, NOT, the cheap, classless pit of pop music and peculiar practices that he makes it out to be. It is a meeting-place for people of discrimination, taste and a wide-open wallet. This is the kind of book that gives our city a bad reputation. It should be banned immediately."
Jan van Ripoff - *Superior Hotels Bulletin, Amsterdam*

"This book should be nailed up on every church door to show what happens to a city where my warnings are not heeded."
John Calvin - *Episcopal Weekly, January 17, 1742*

"For once I agree. Another fatwa is in order."
A. Khomeini - *Iranian Free Press Agency*

"This book proves what I have been saying for years. We should have done something about Amsterdam long ago. You see what happened to the Berlin Wall when such subversive literature went unchecked?"
Nikolai Streptokoki - *K G B Veterans Newsletter, June 5, 1993*

"The author is a communist, anarchist and homosexual. I suggest a pinpoint strike on Amsterdam. Too many bicycle repair shops capable of producing nuclear weapons."
CIA Quarterly - *June 5, 1993*

"This book is long overdue. If it had been published sooner it would have saved me a long trip for Indonesian take-out."
Christopher Columbus - *Travellers' Gazette, December 7, 1505*